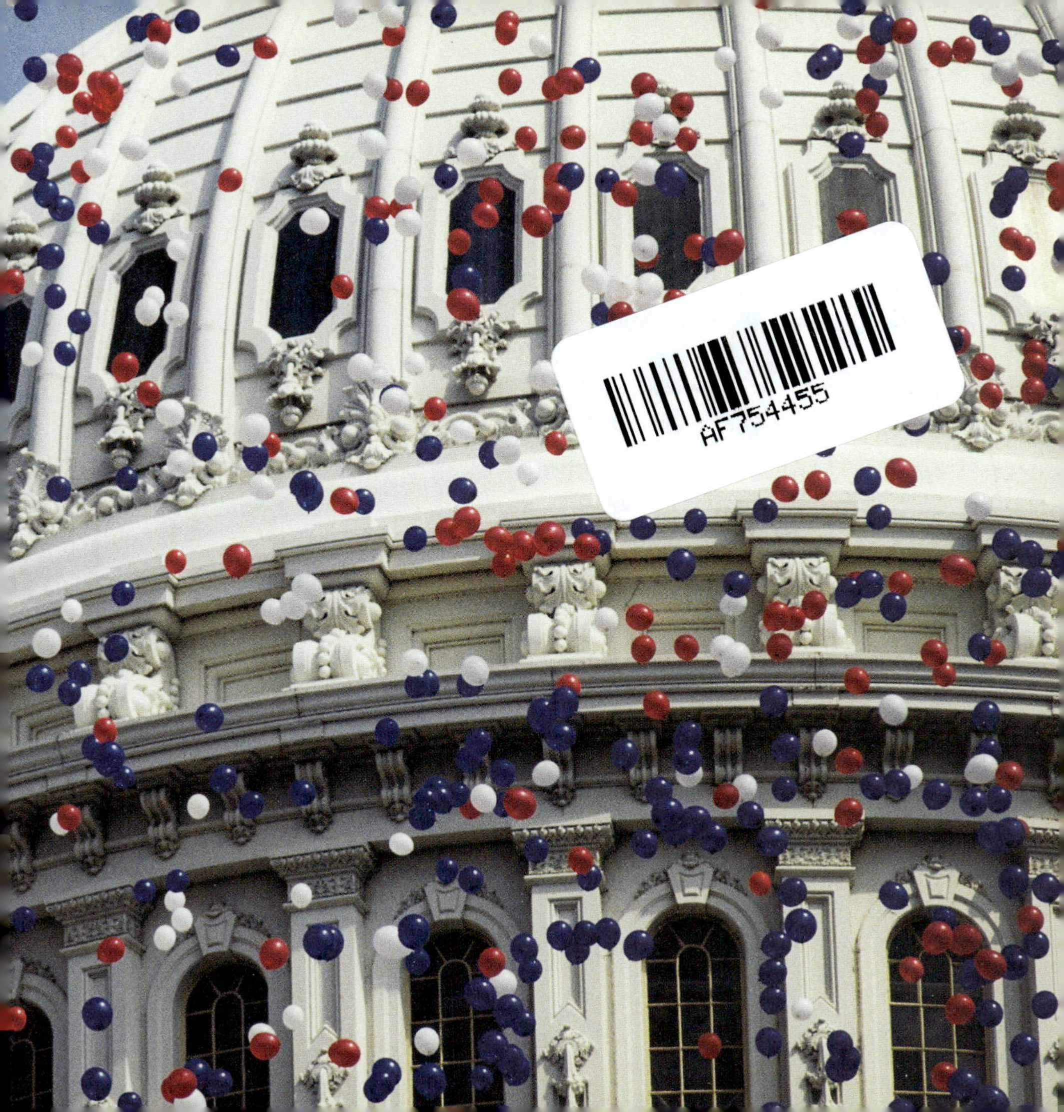

WASHINGTON, DC

INSPIRE US

GOOD NIGHT BOOKS

© 2020 Good Night Books
ISBN: 978-1-60219-945-3

The Inspire Us series is an imprint of Good Night Books, LLC.

All rights reserved. No part of this publication may be reproduced or transmitted in any form or by any means, electronic, mechanical, photocopying, recording, or otherwise, without prior written consent of the publisher.
For more information, please contact the publisher.
www.goodnightbooks.com
Printed in China.

The Inspire Us series was created by Adam Gamble.
Publisher: Mark Jasper.
Associate Publisher: Apaarjeet Chopra.
Lead Photo Editor for *Washington, DC, Inspire Us*: Adam Clear.

Dedicated to Teddy Steere.

PREFACE

Welcome to the Inspire Us series, a photographic celebration of community. Whether a local community based on place—such as a region, city, state, or country—or a dispersed community based on shared interests—like hobbies, activities, or fan groups—these books celebrate with mesmerizing images from myriad photographers.

Since 2005, Good Night Books has published a popular line of celebratory children's books based on places and themes: the Good Night Our World series. We know from firsthand experience that books can inspire children and their families to better understand and value their communities, even to take action and get involved in making our shared world a better place. Similarly, we hope the Inspire Us series will motivate you, our audience, to more deeply appreciate community.

As noted by the Japanese photographer and philosopher Daisaku Ikeda, photography is a universal language that communicates without words. Photographs transcend differences such as nationality, ethnicity, age, gender, and background, conveying that which cannot be articulated. Perhaps this is why photography can be so emotionally expressive and evocative. It is also why we have placed the captions and credits for each photo in separate sections in the back of this book, so that words do not detract from the visuals.

In curating images for each title in this series, we use three principal criteria. First, we look for artistically impactful images that express strong ideas, perspectives, and feelings. Second, each must capture and convey something essential to the theme of the book, so that the collective result is a broad and rich exploration of the subject. Third, and most importantly, each image must have the potential to inspire.

The word inspire means to fill one with the urge or desire to feel or to do something, especially something creative. The word derives from the Latin *inspirare*, which means "to breathe into." It also shares a root with the English word "spirit," which comes from the Latin *spirare*. Thus, "to inspire" evokes the idea of "breathing life into," or "filling with spirit," or even "filling with divine spirit." We at Good Night Books believe in inspiration, specifically the inspiration to contribute to a better world. Walt Whitman shares this sentiment sublimely in his poem "Song of the Open Road":

Gently, but with undeniable will, divesting myself of the holds that would hold me.

I inhale great draughts of space,

The east and the west are mine, and the north and the south are mine.

I am larger, better than I thought,

I did not know I held so much goodness.

All seems beautiful to me, I can repeat over to men and women,

You have done such good to me I would do the same to you.

We thank you for joining us in the Inspire Us series. We wish you the best of journeys.

—Good Night Books

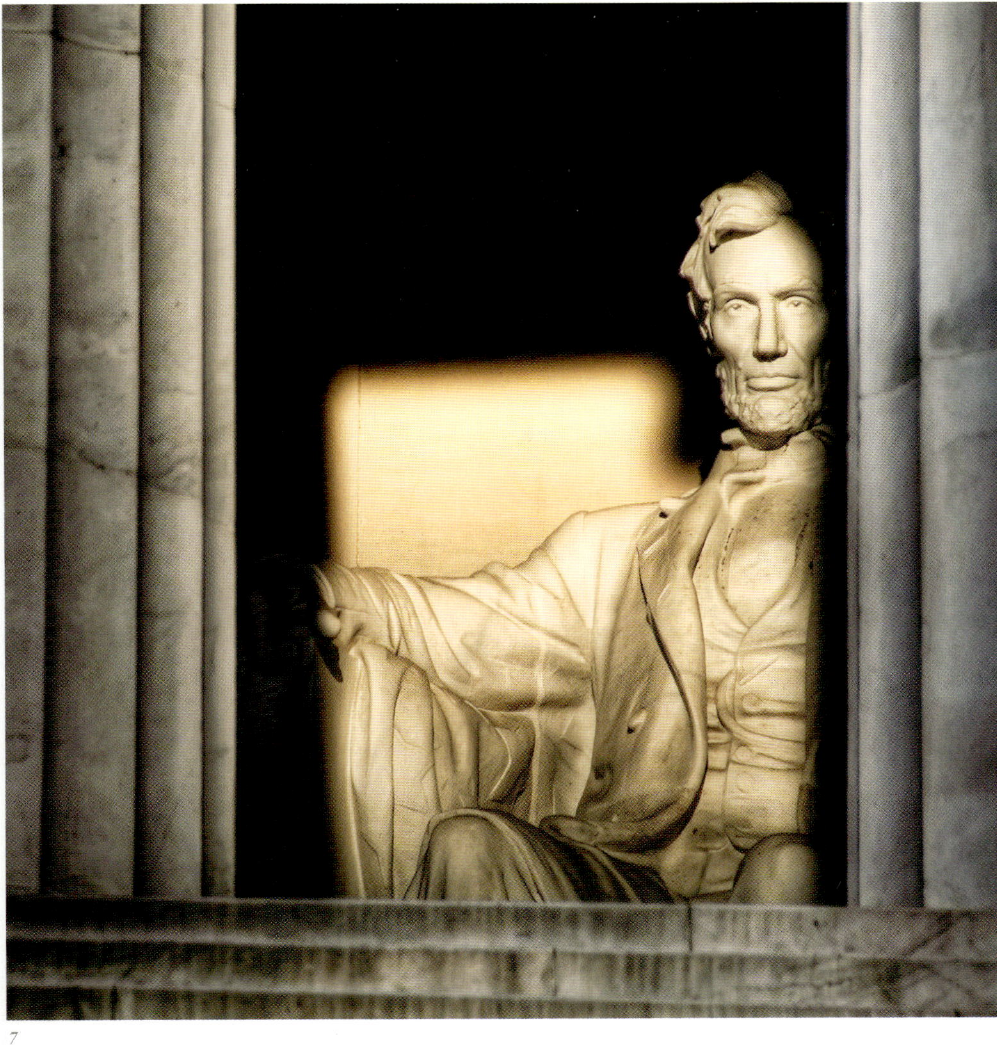

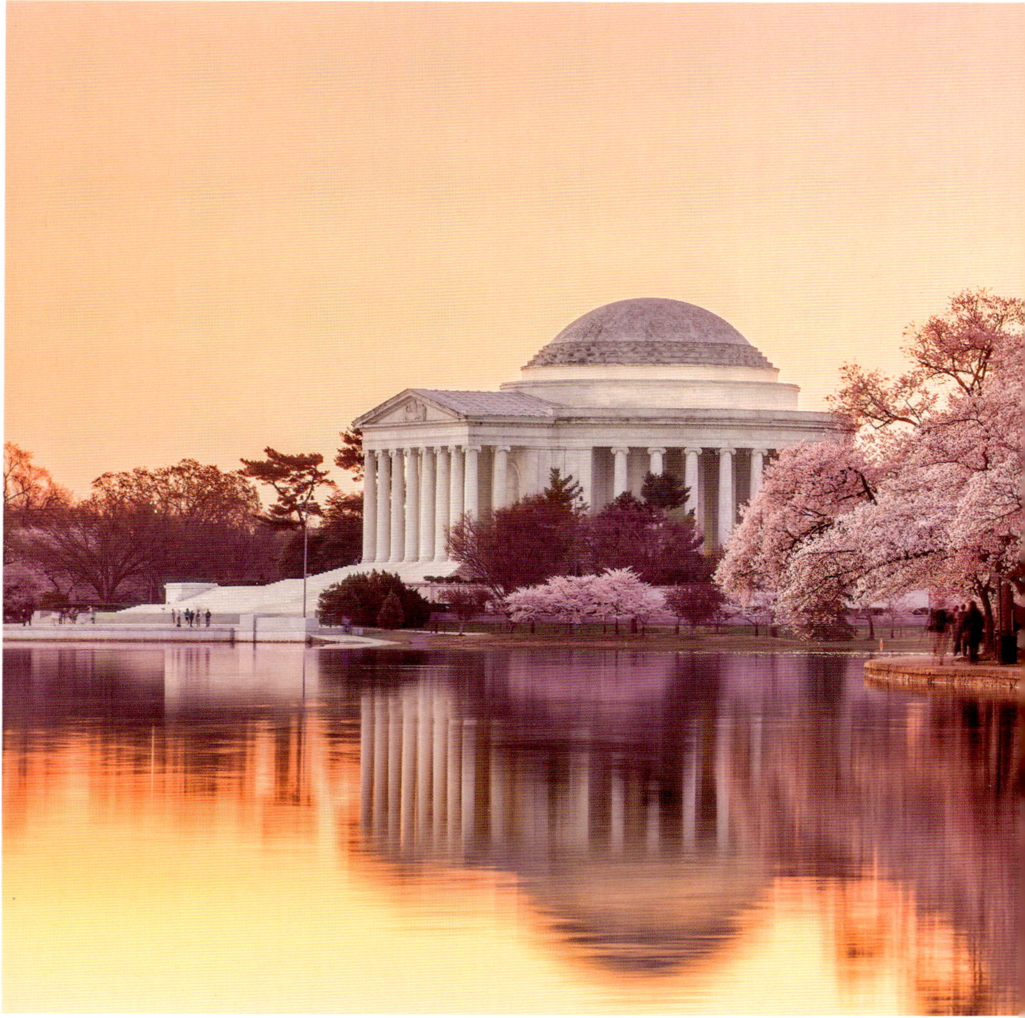

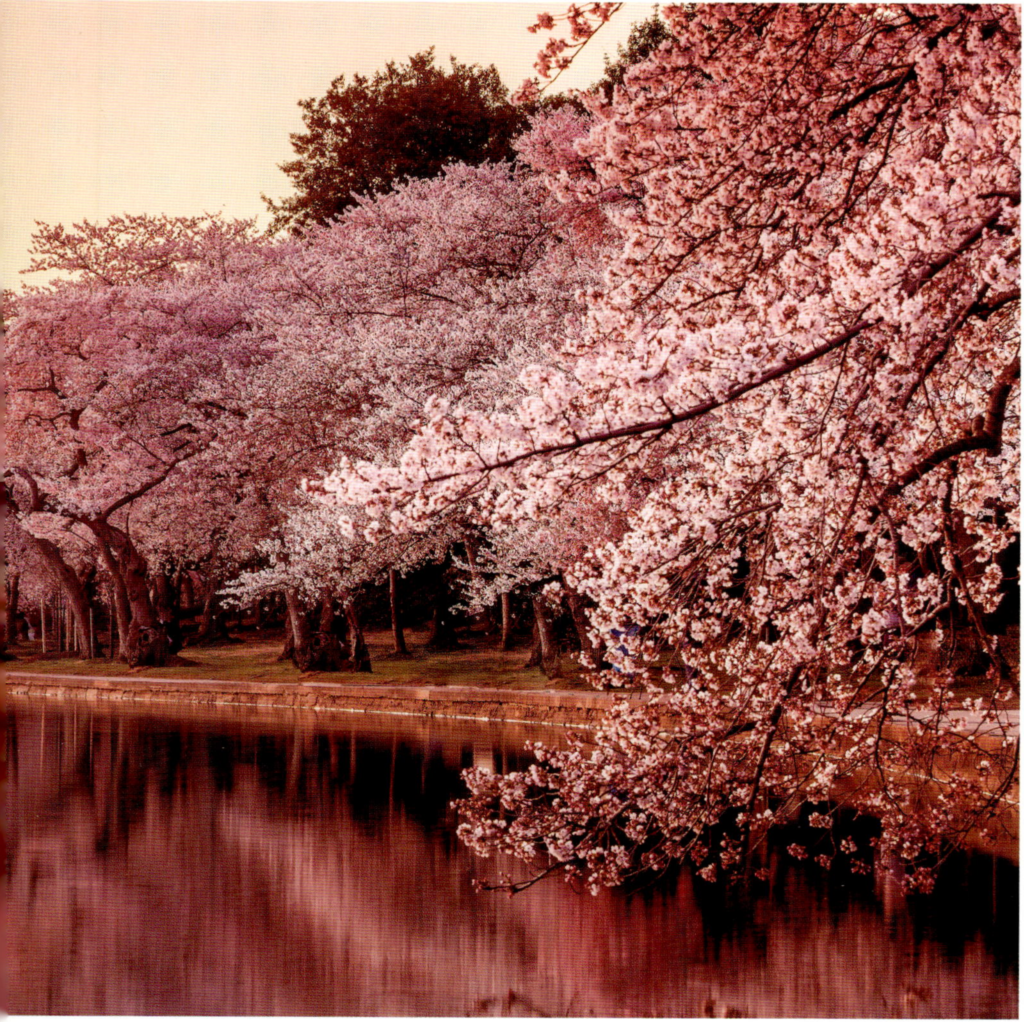

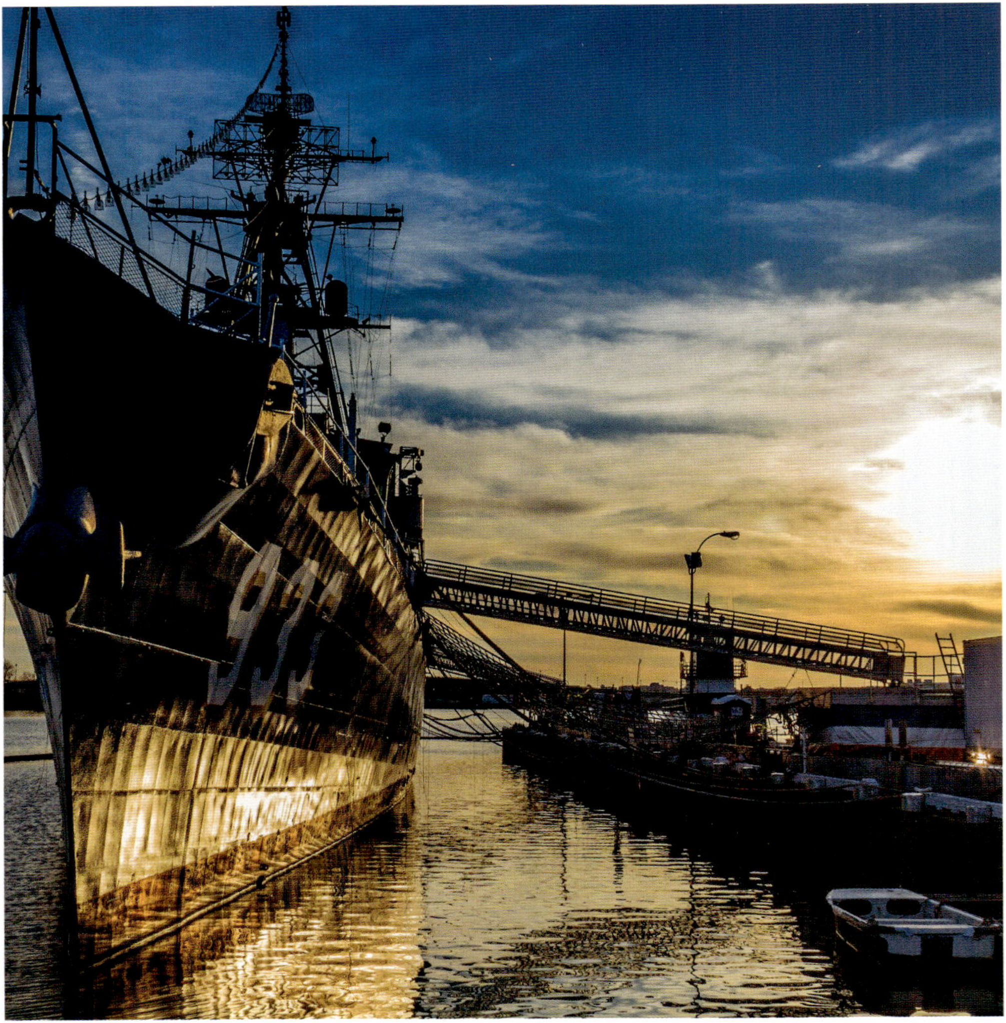

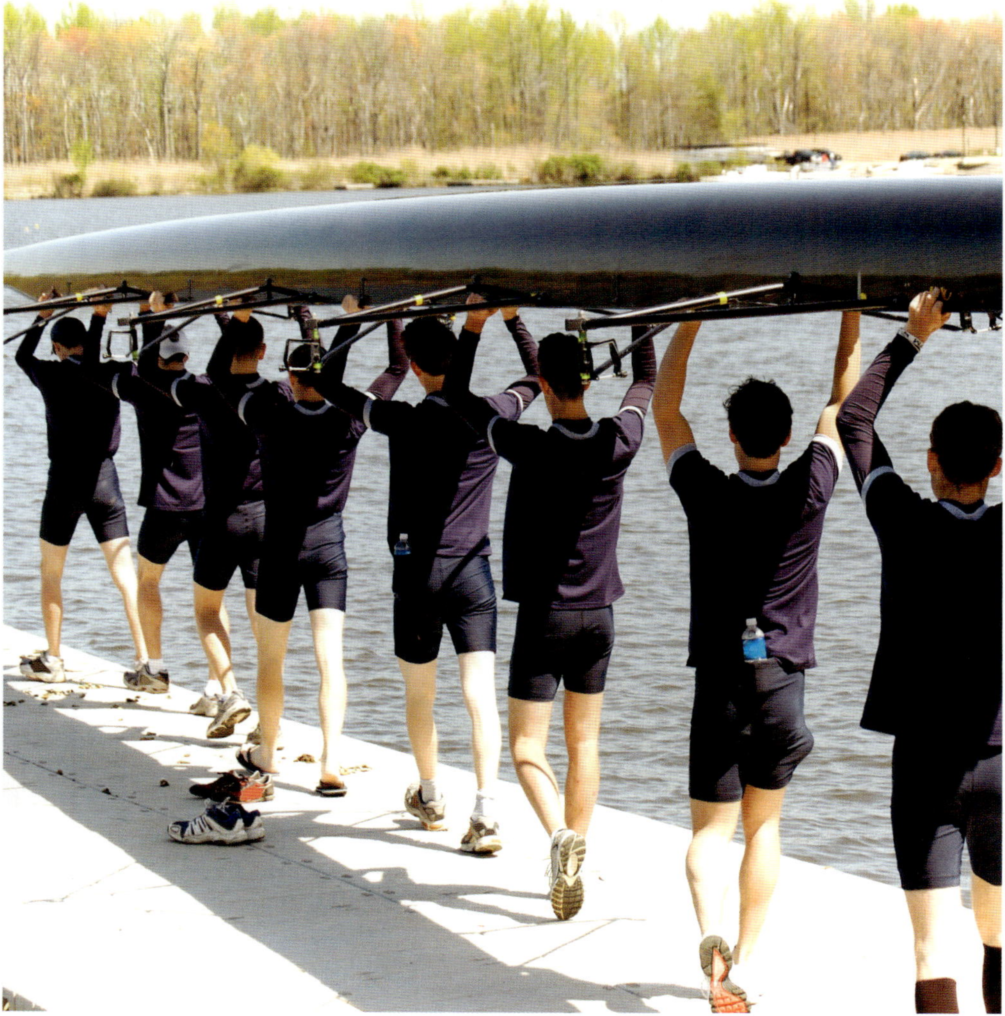

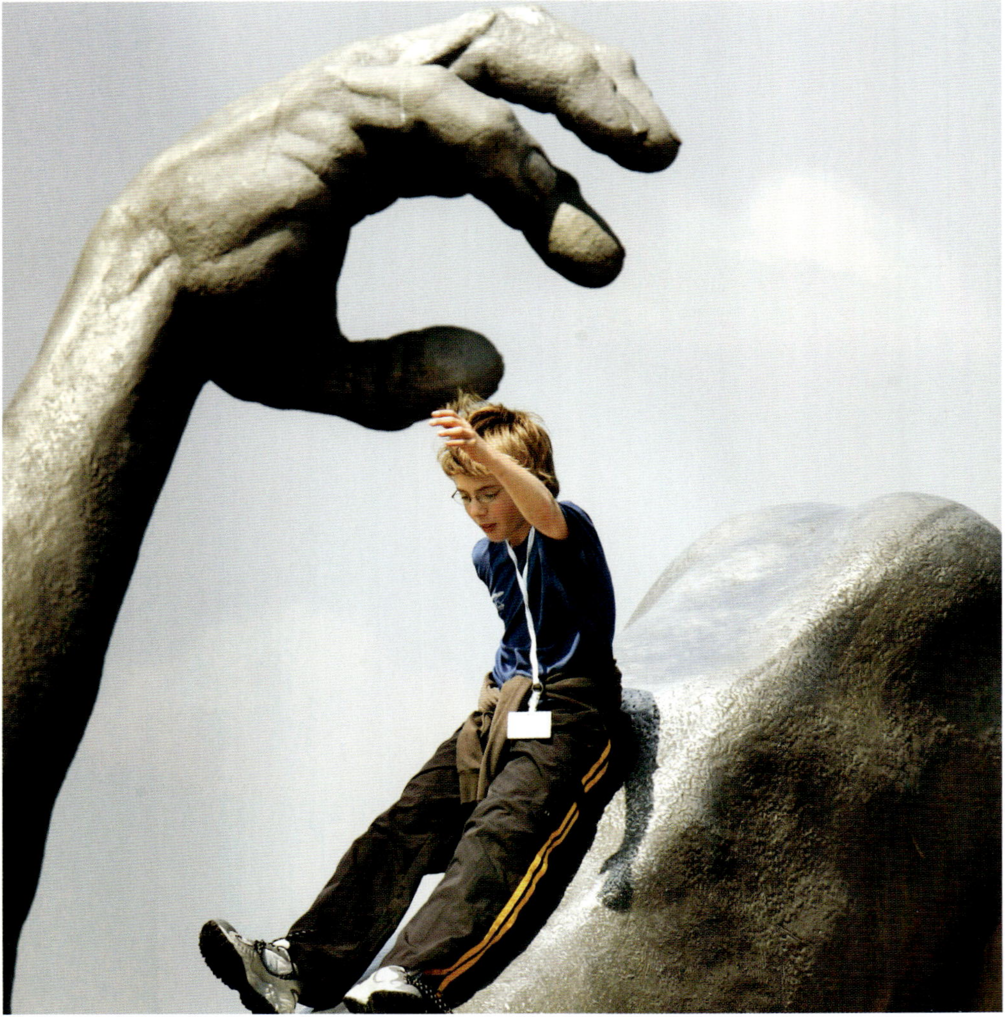

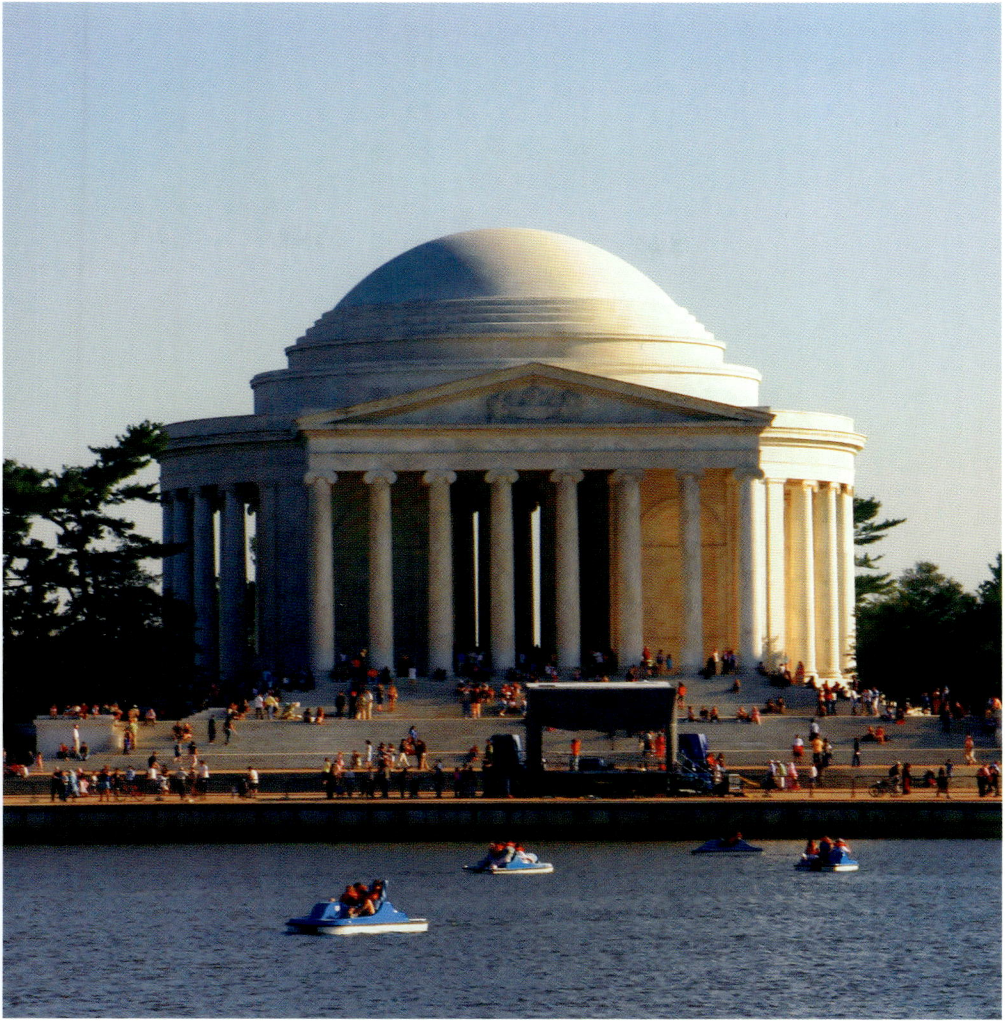

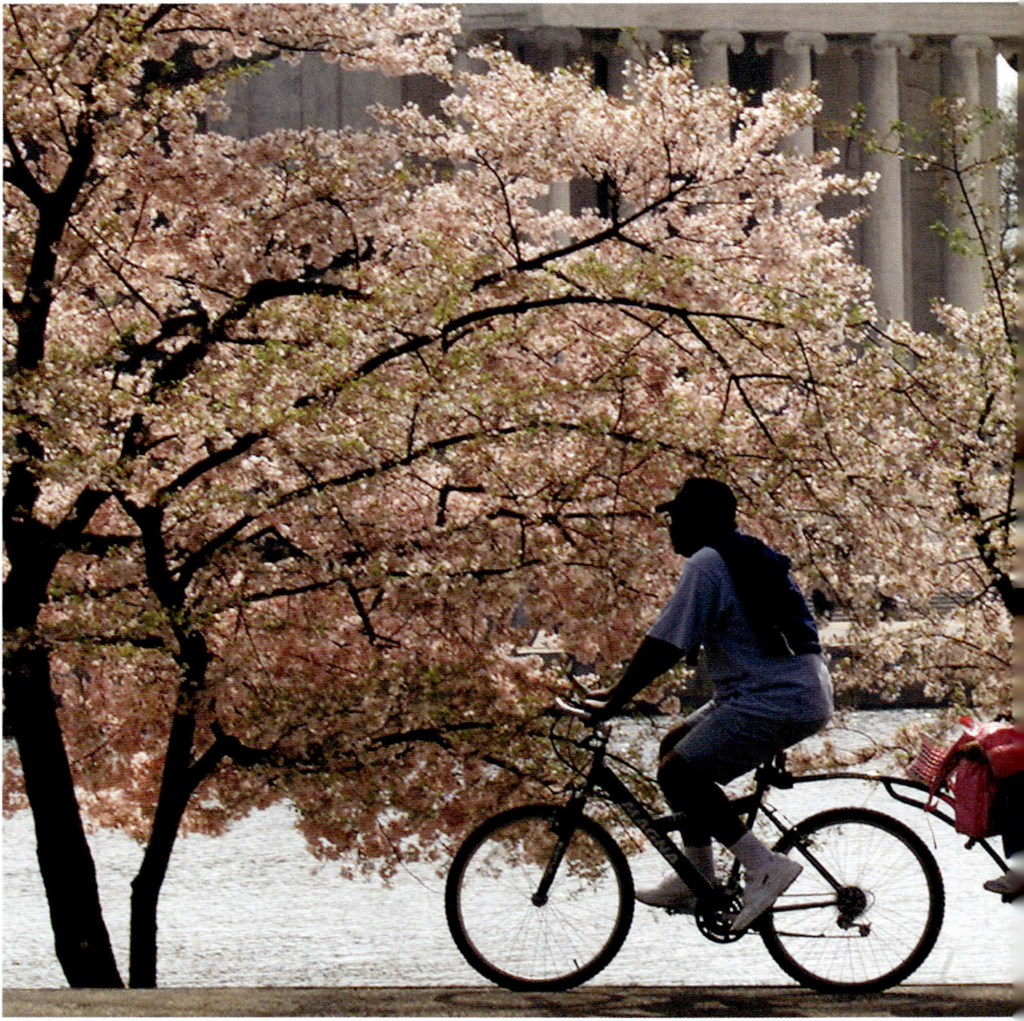

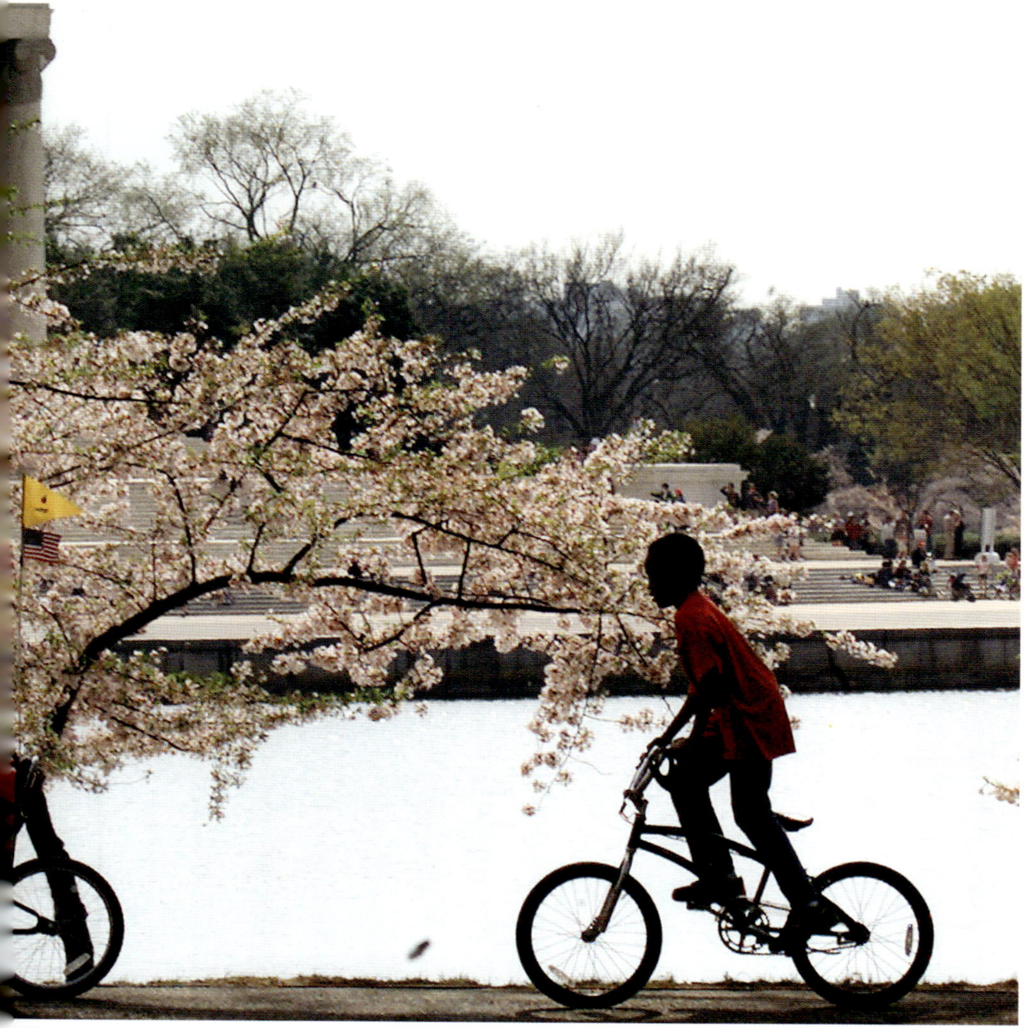

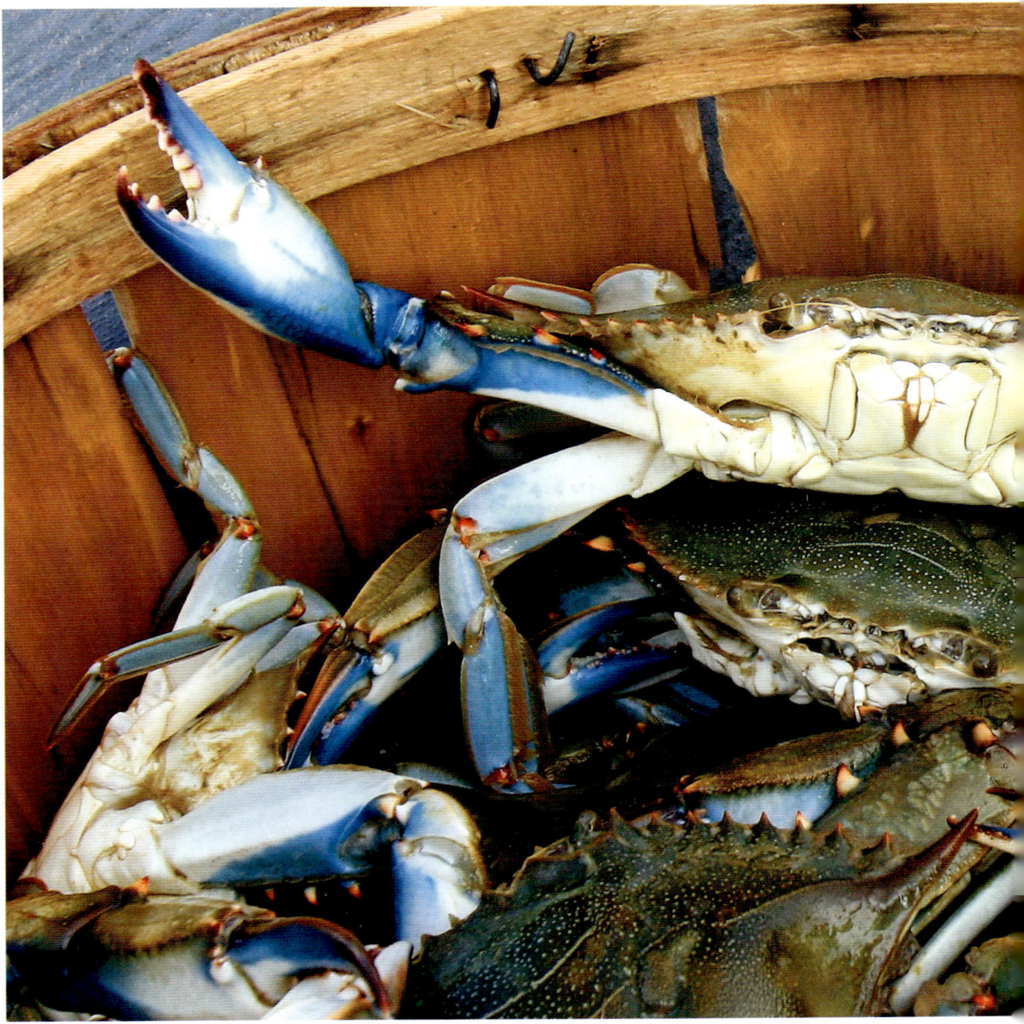

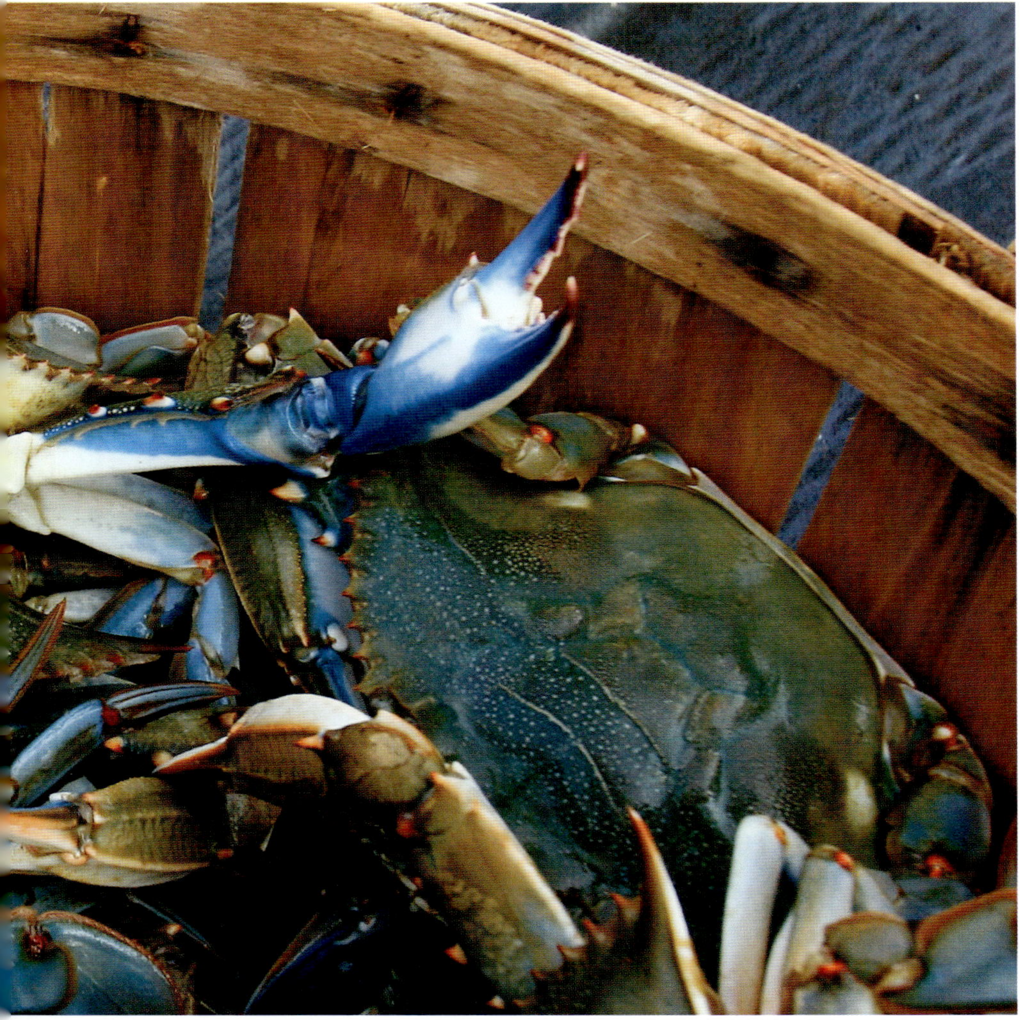

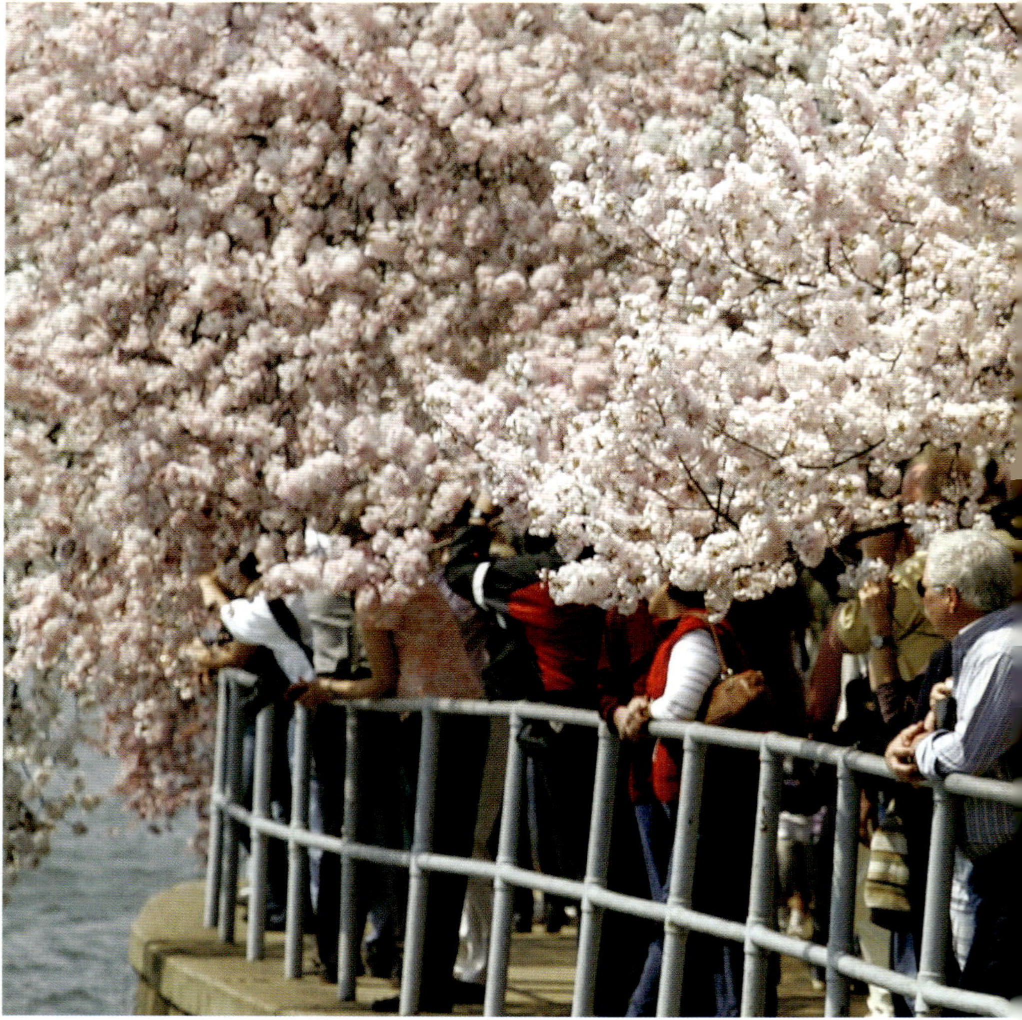

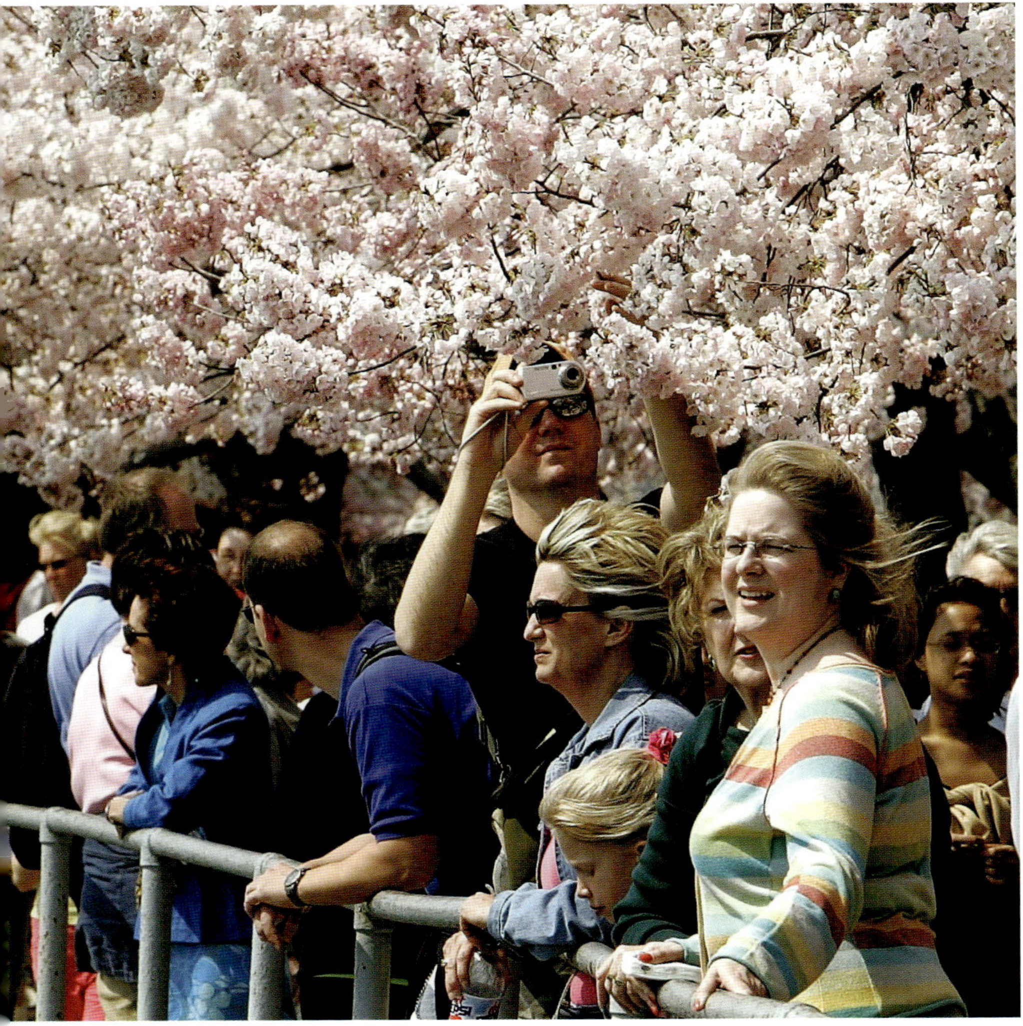

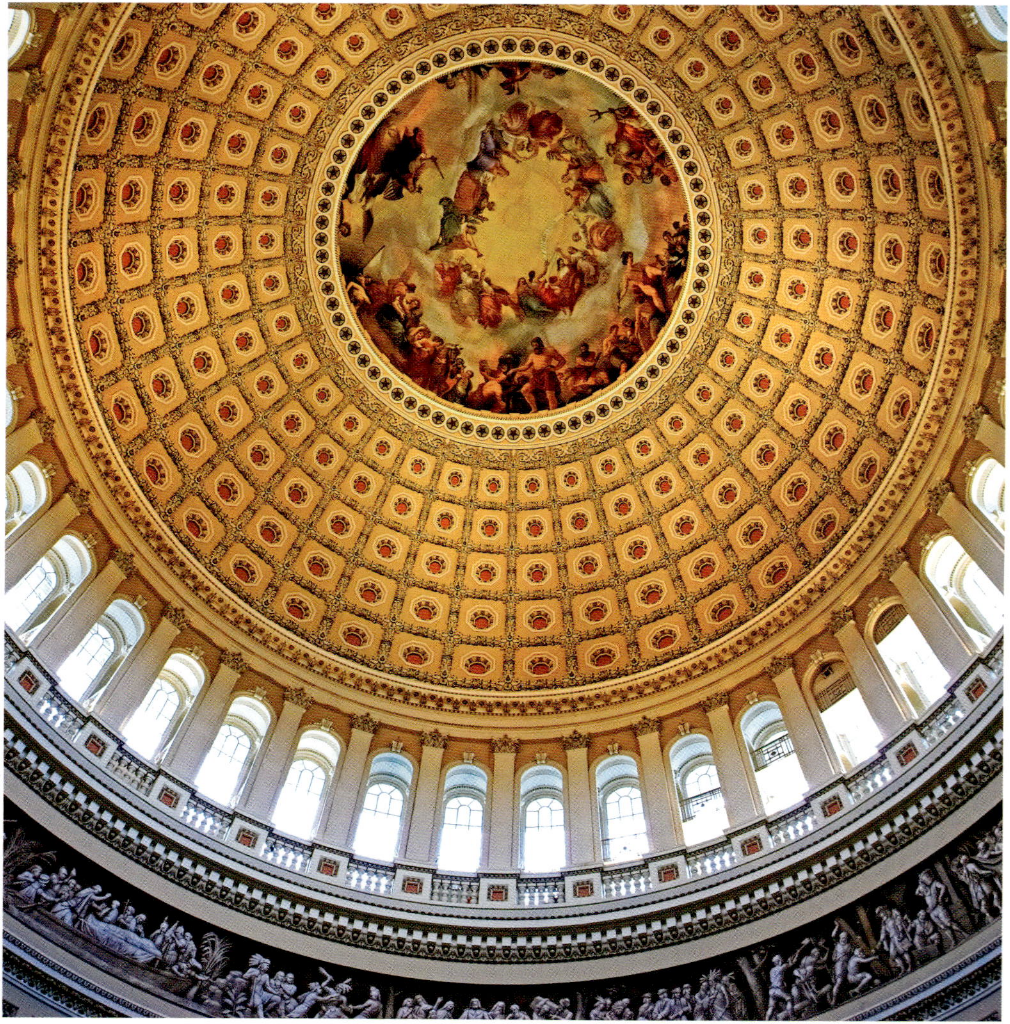

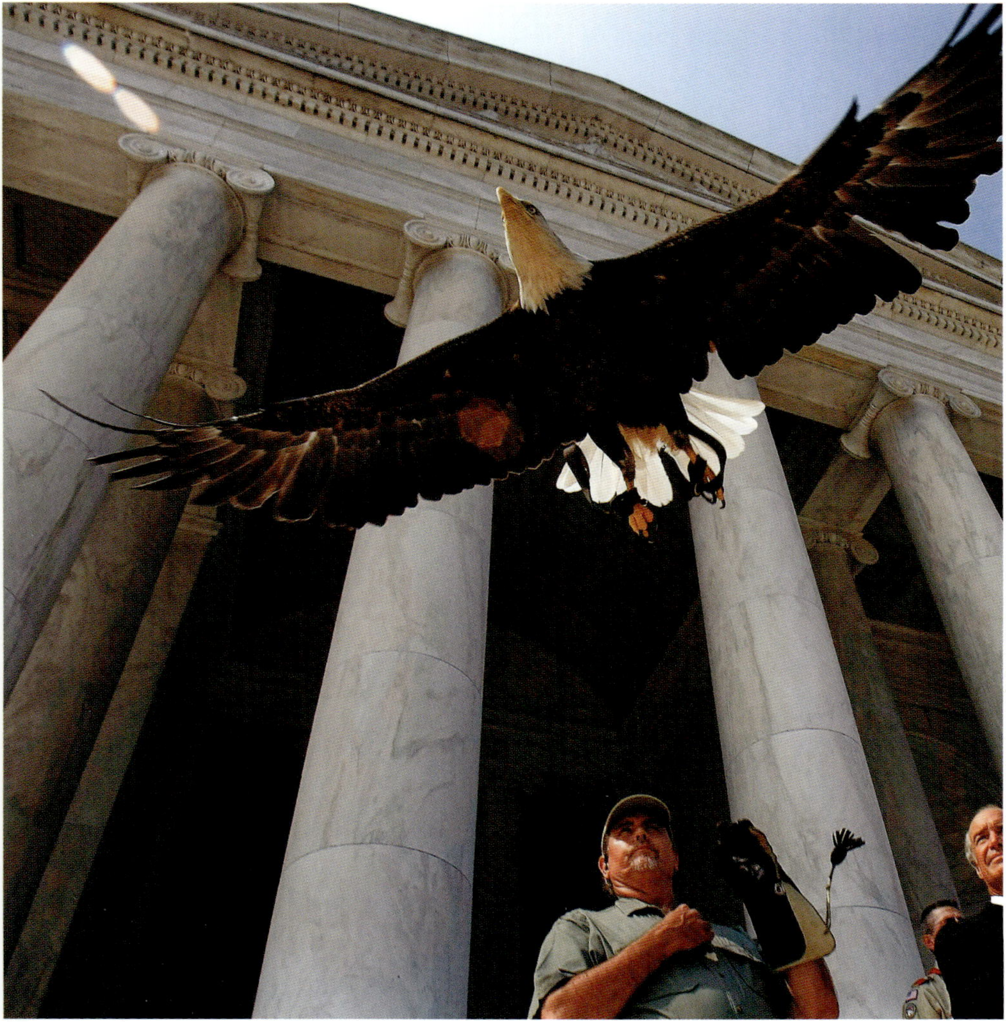

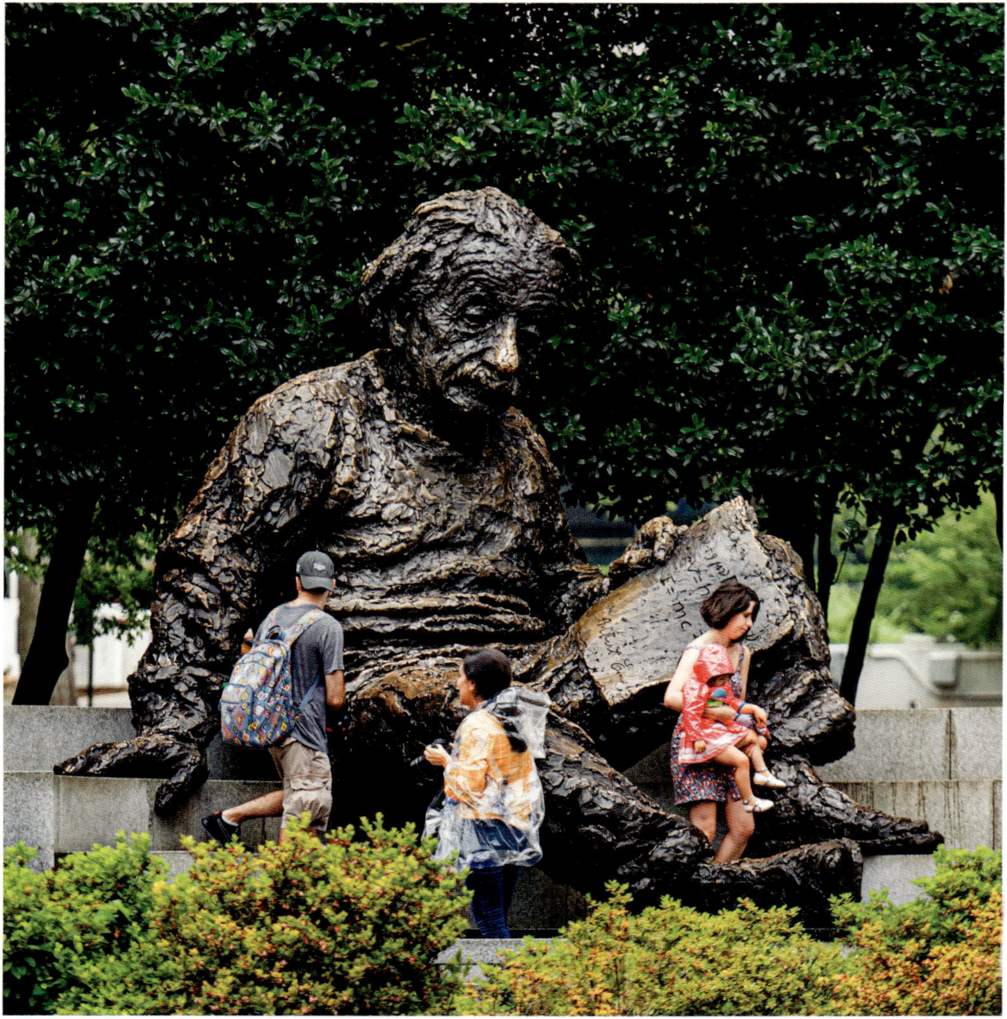
E=mc

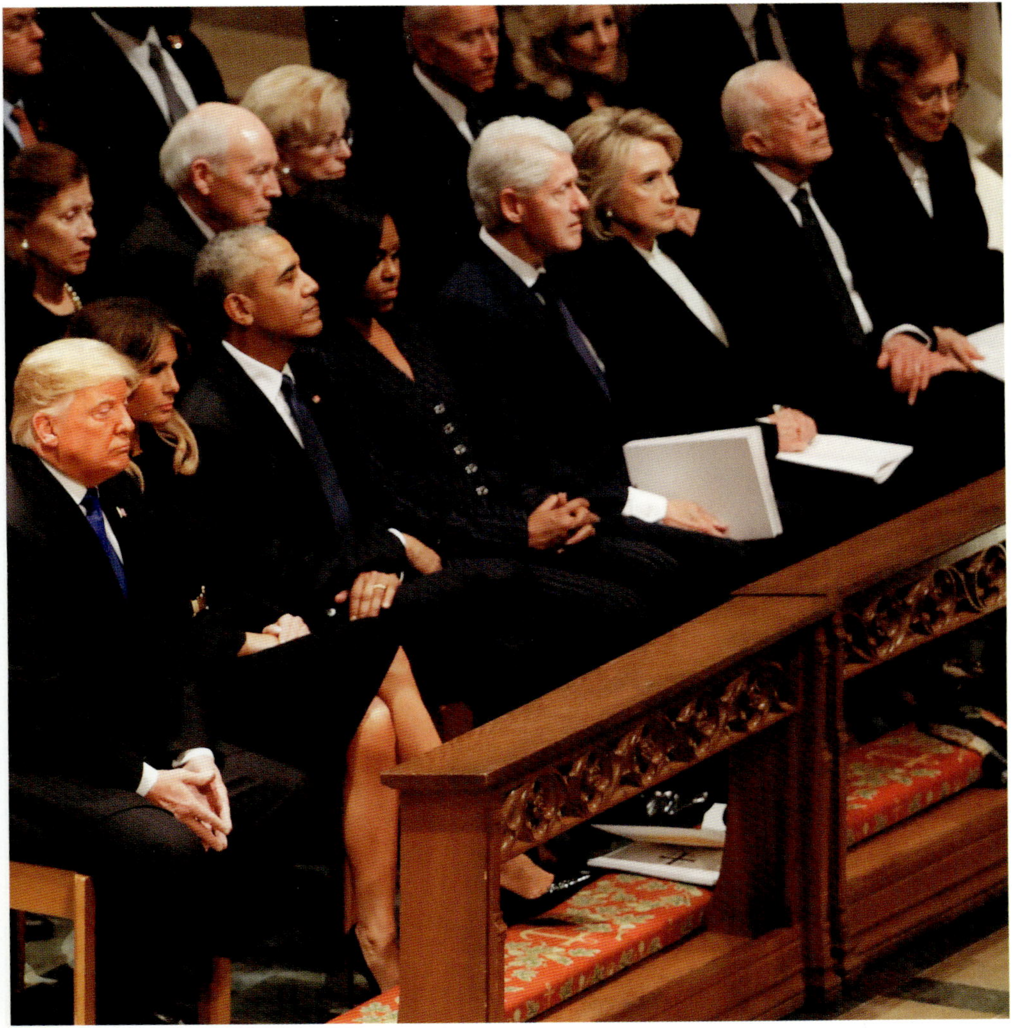

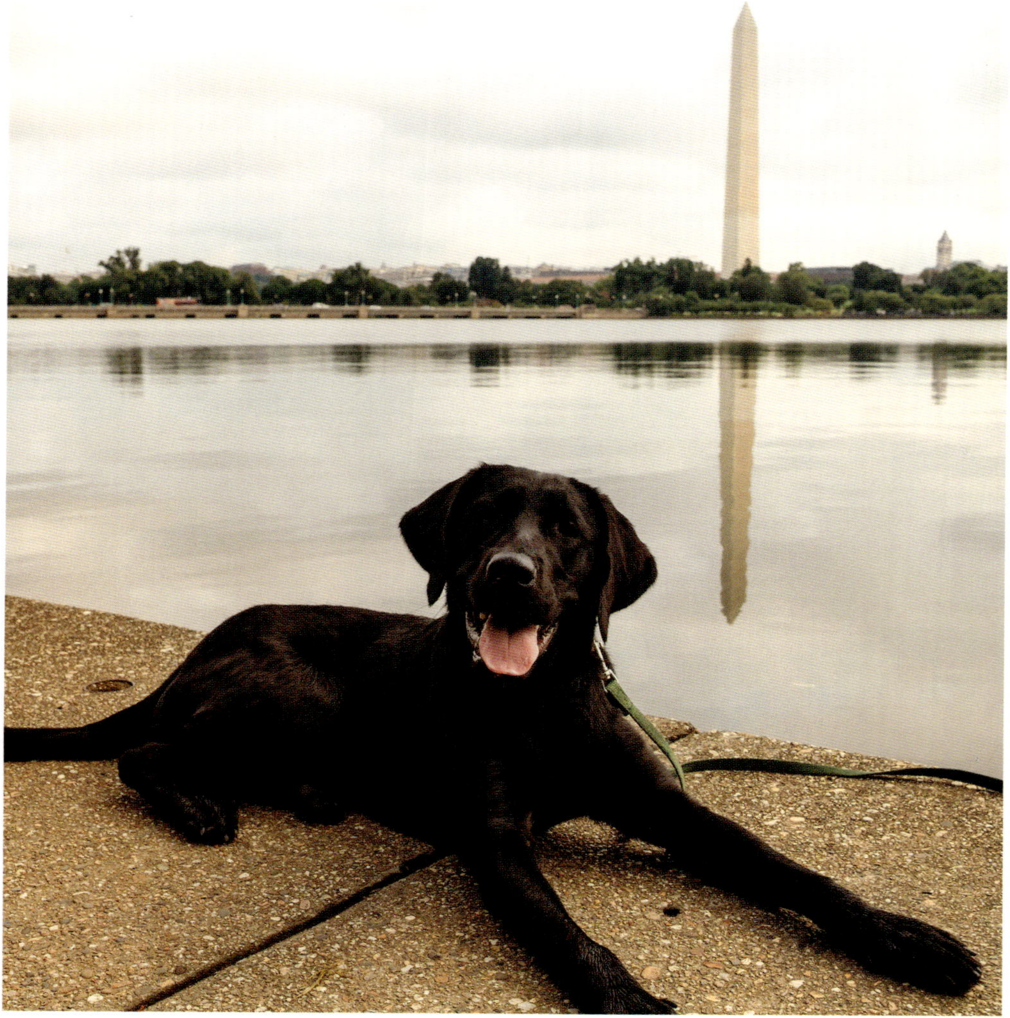

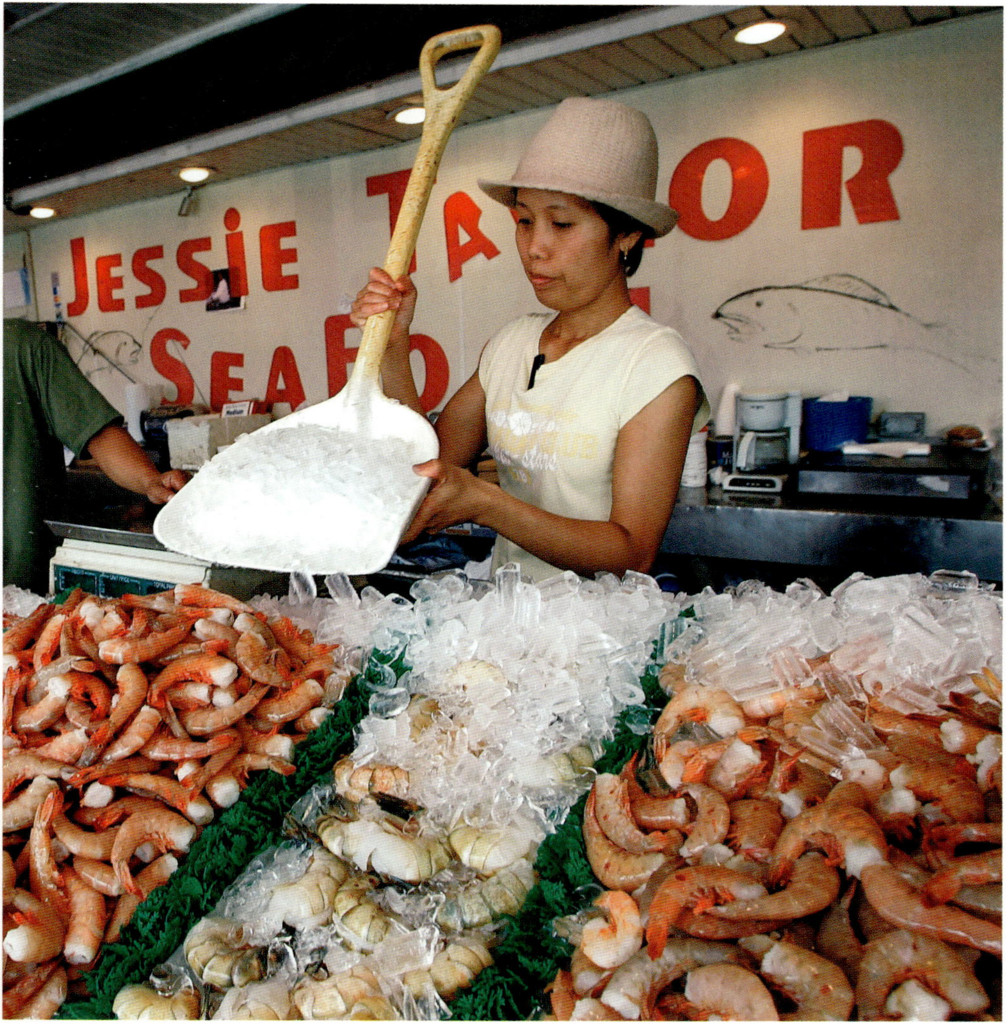
JESSIE

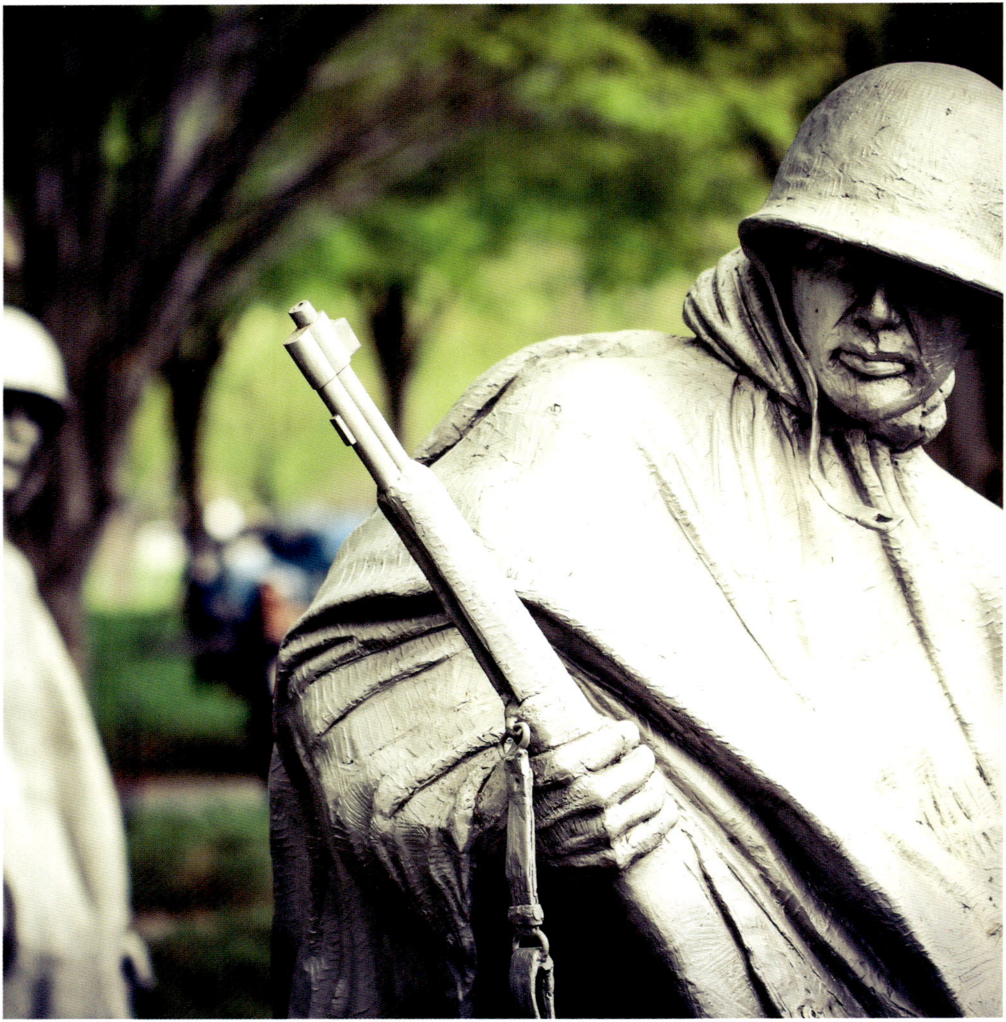

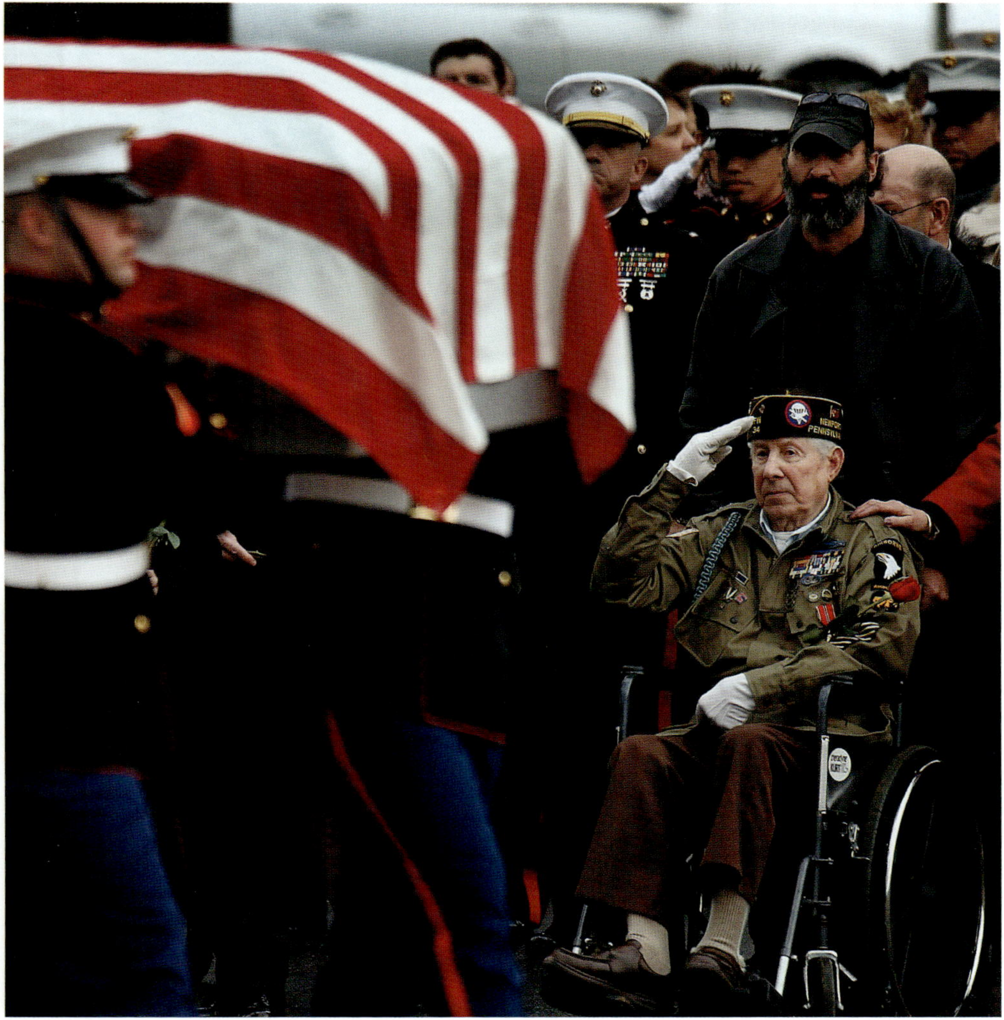

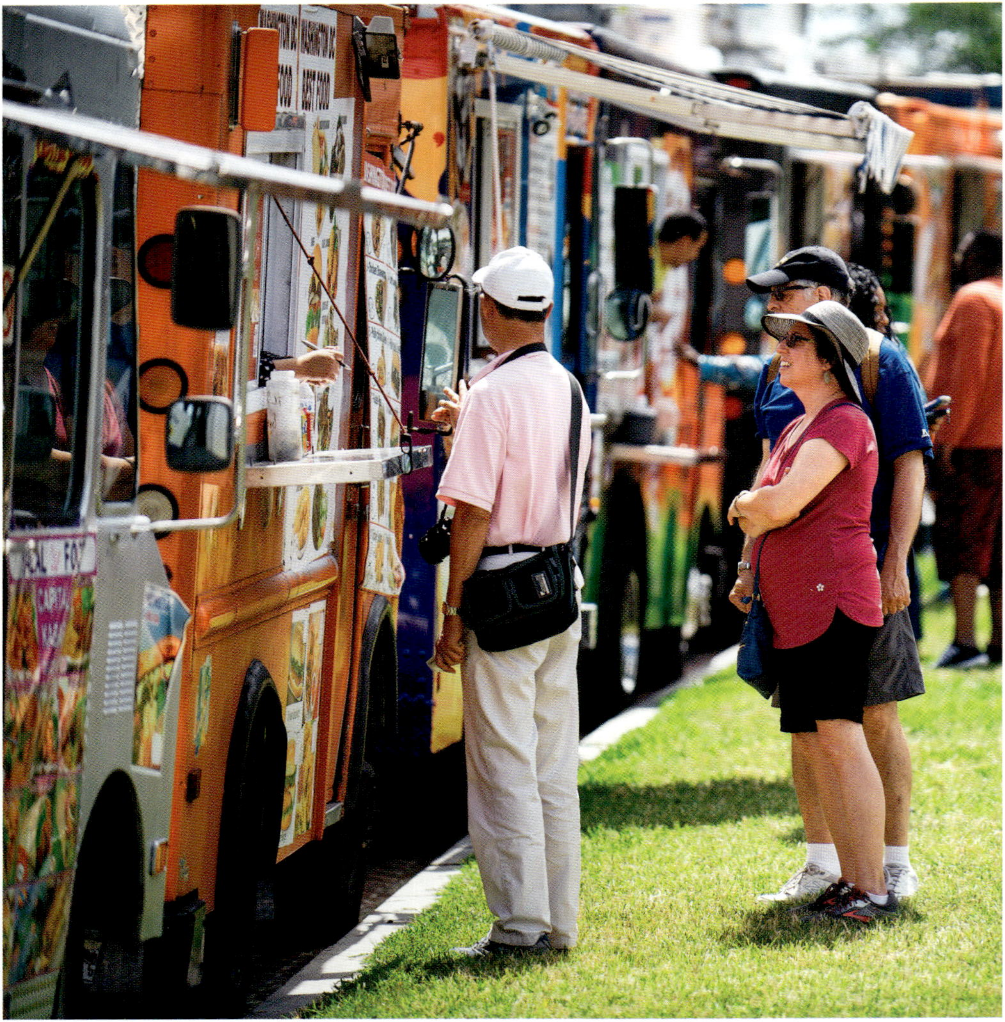
WASHINGTON DC
BEST FOOD

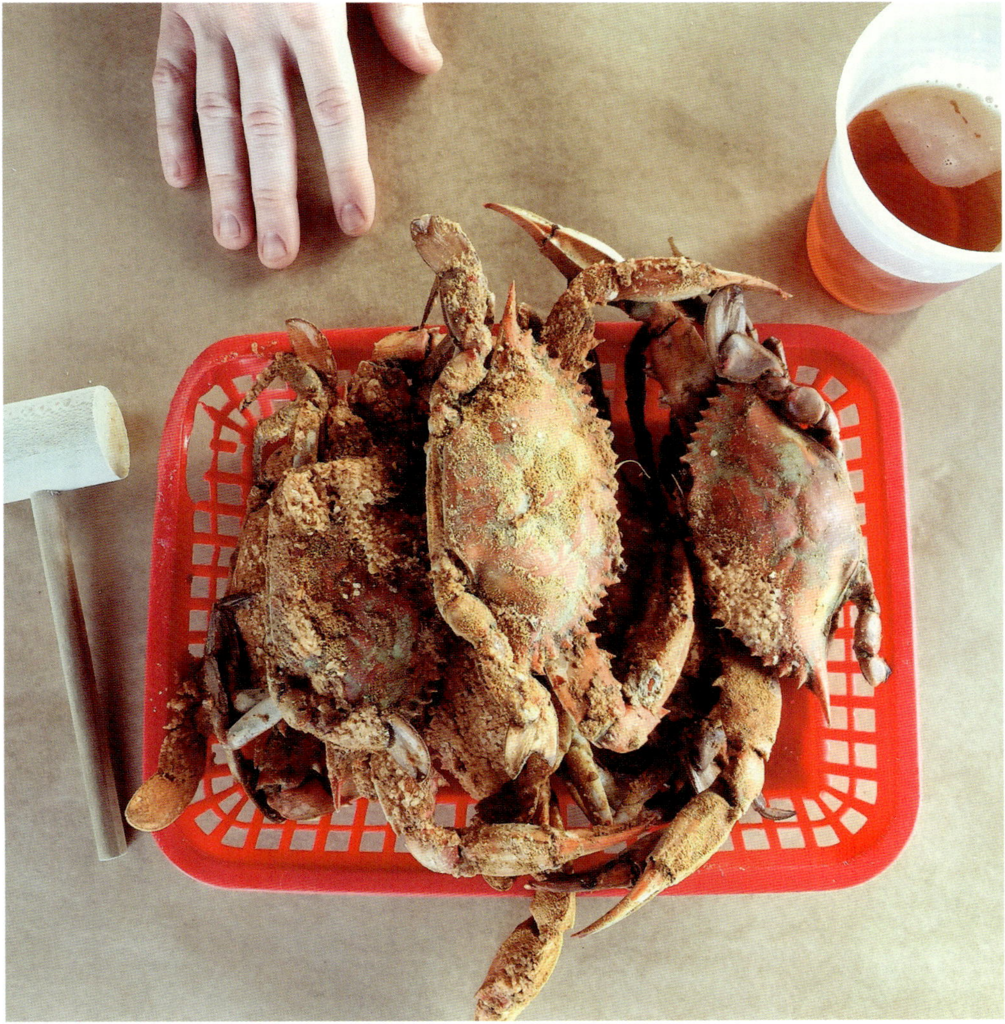

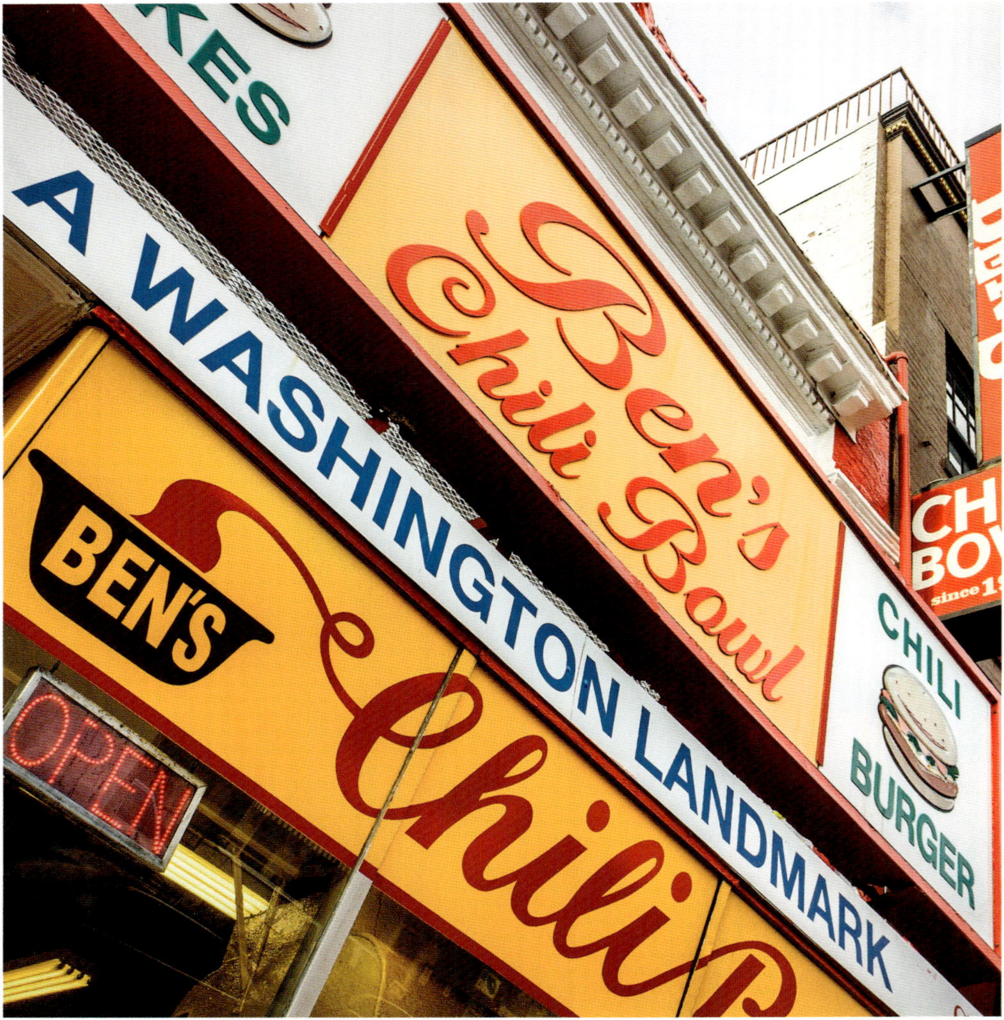
A WASHINGTON LANDMARK
Ben's Chili Bowl
BEN'S
Chili
OPEN
CHILI BURGER

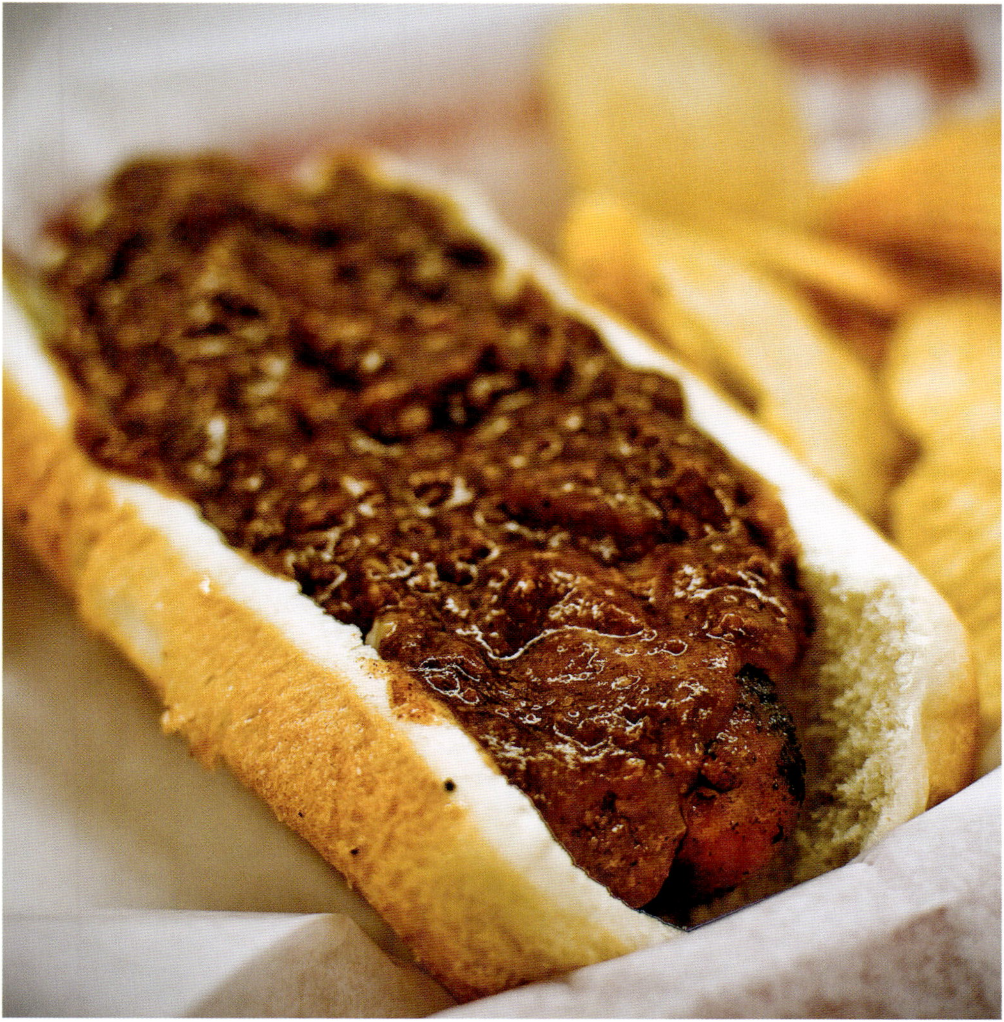

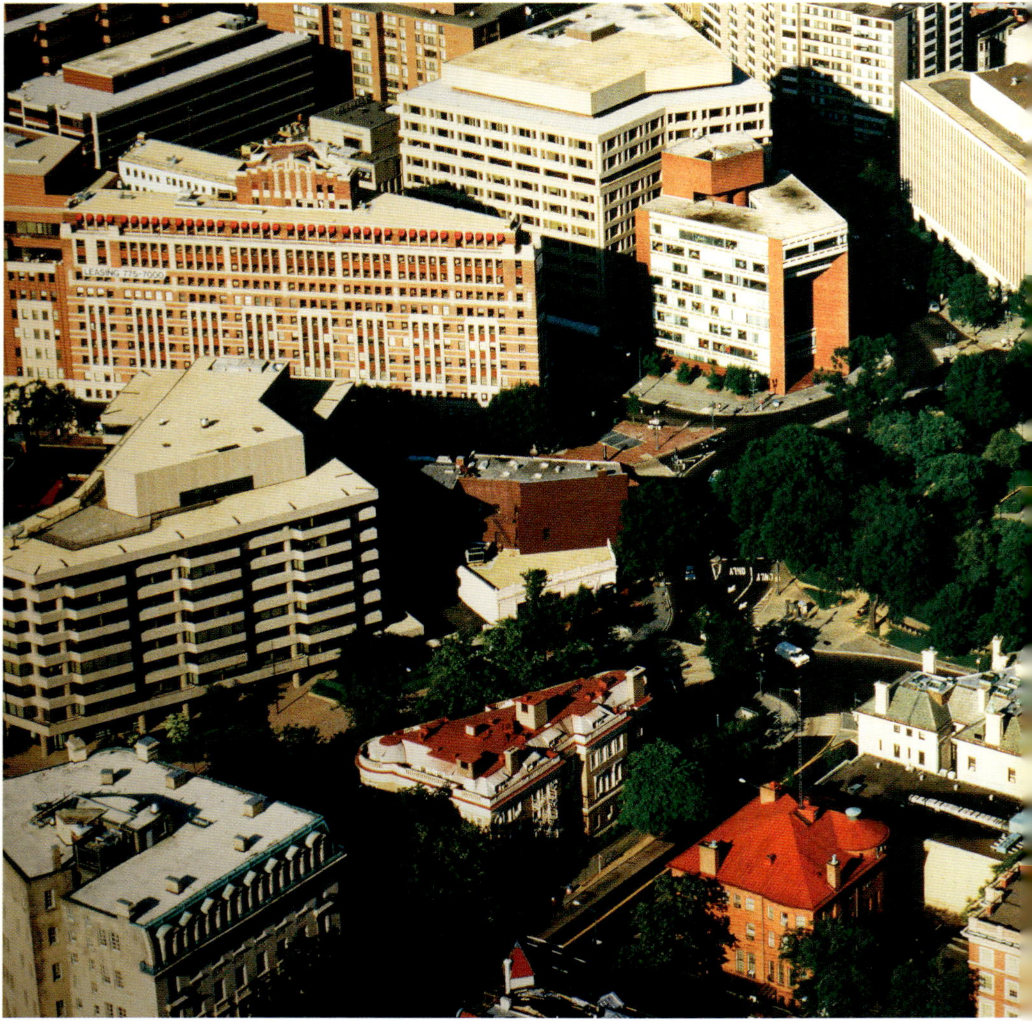
LEASING 775-7000

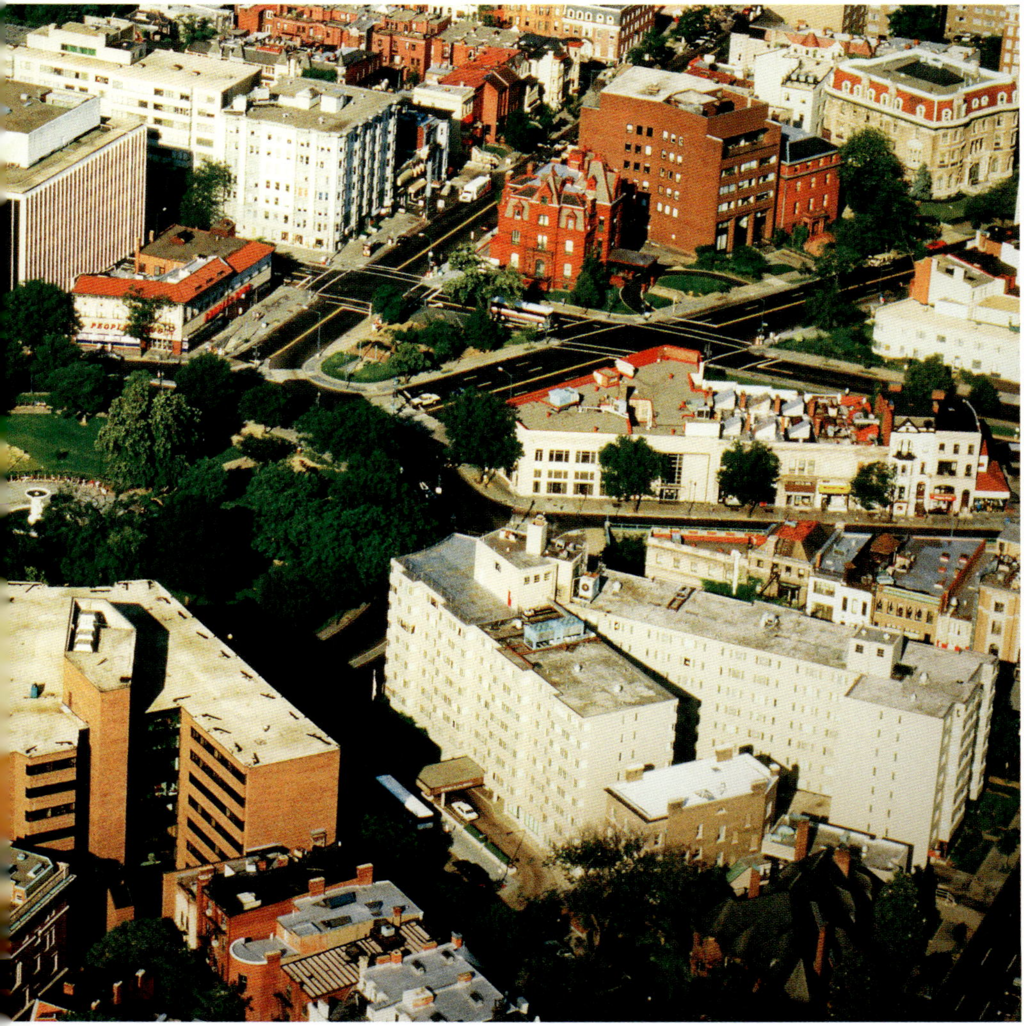

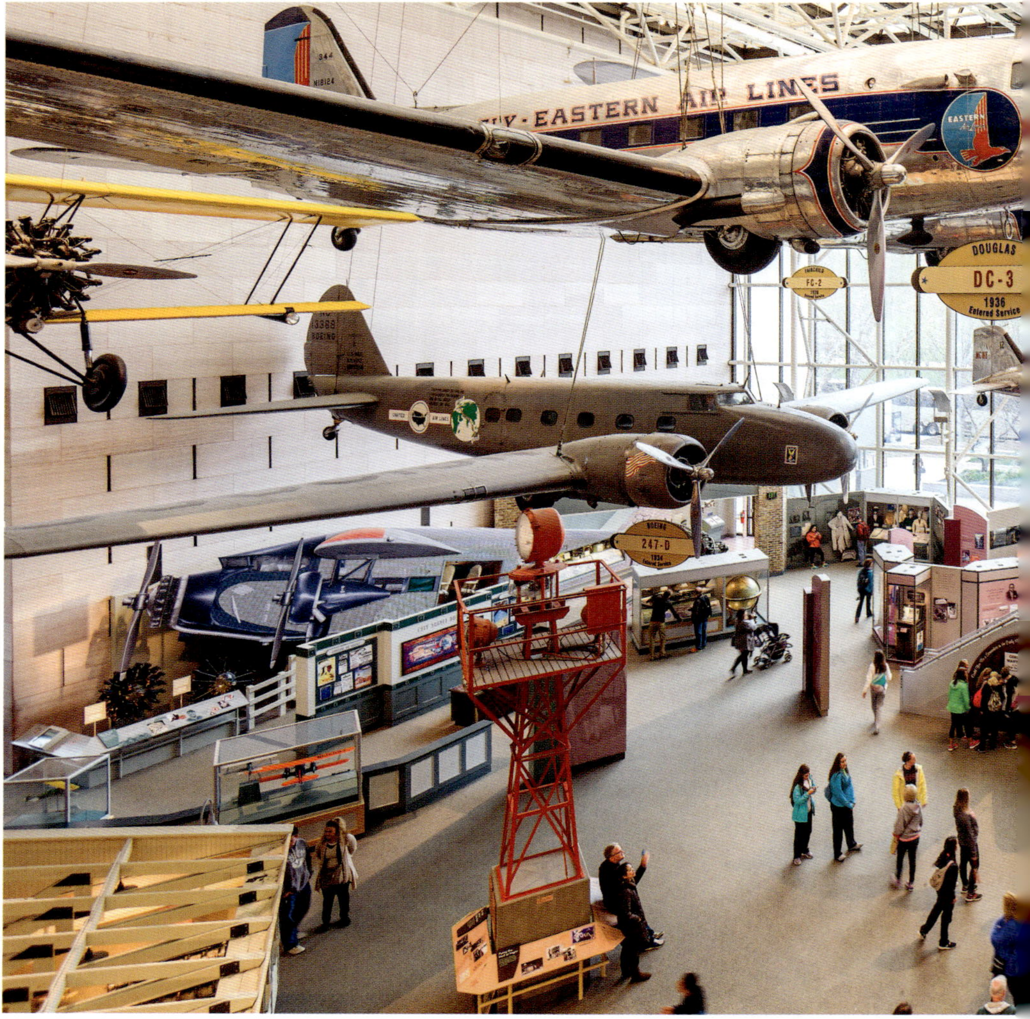
EASTERN AIR LINES
DOUGLAS
DC-3
1936
Entered Service
BOEING
247-D
1934
Entered Service

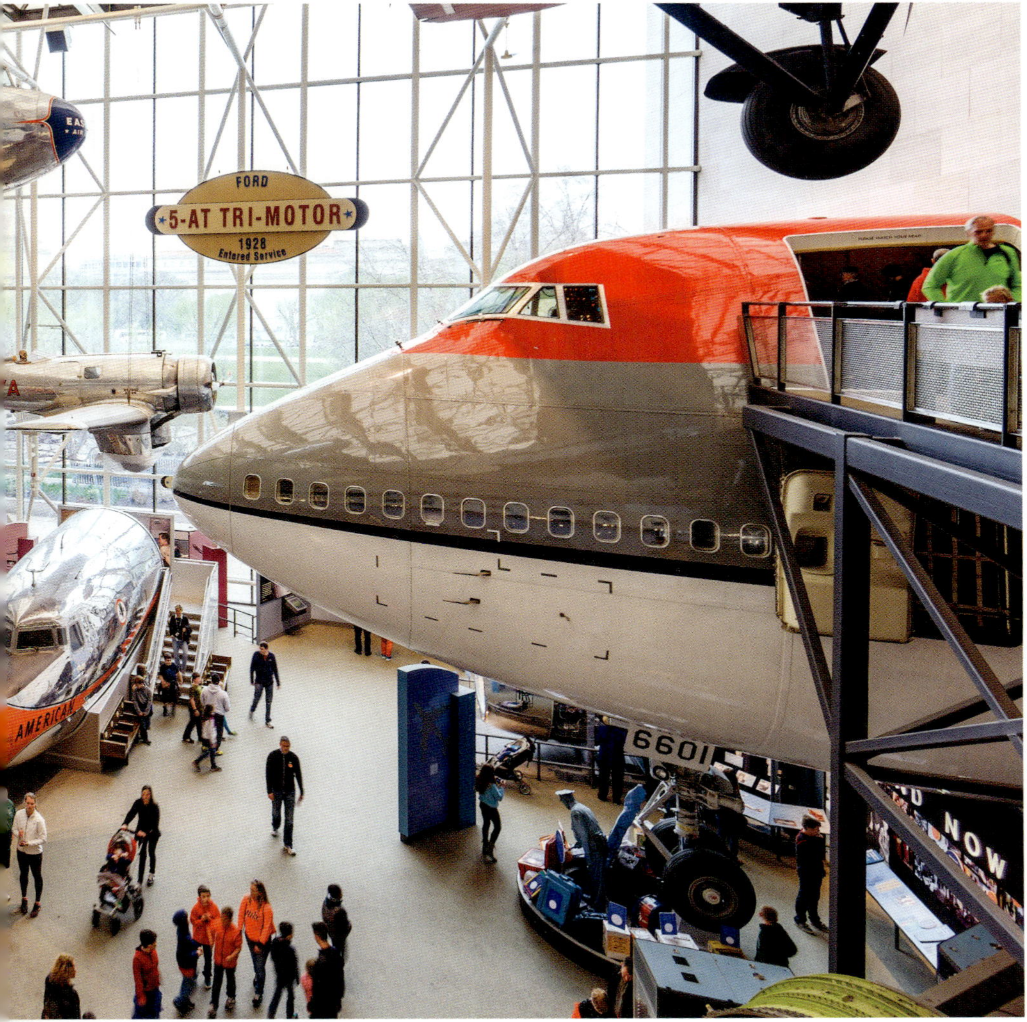
FORD
5-AT TRI-MOTOR
1928
Entered Service
AMERICAN
6601
NOW

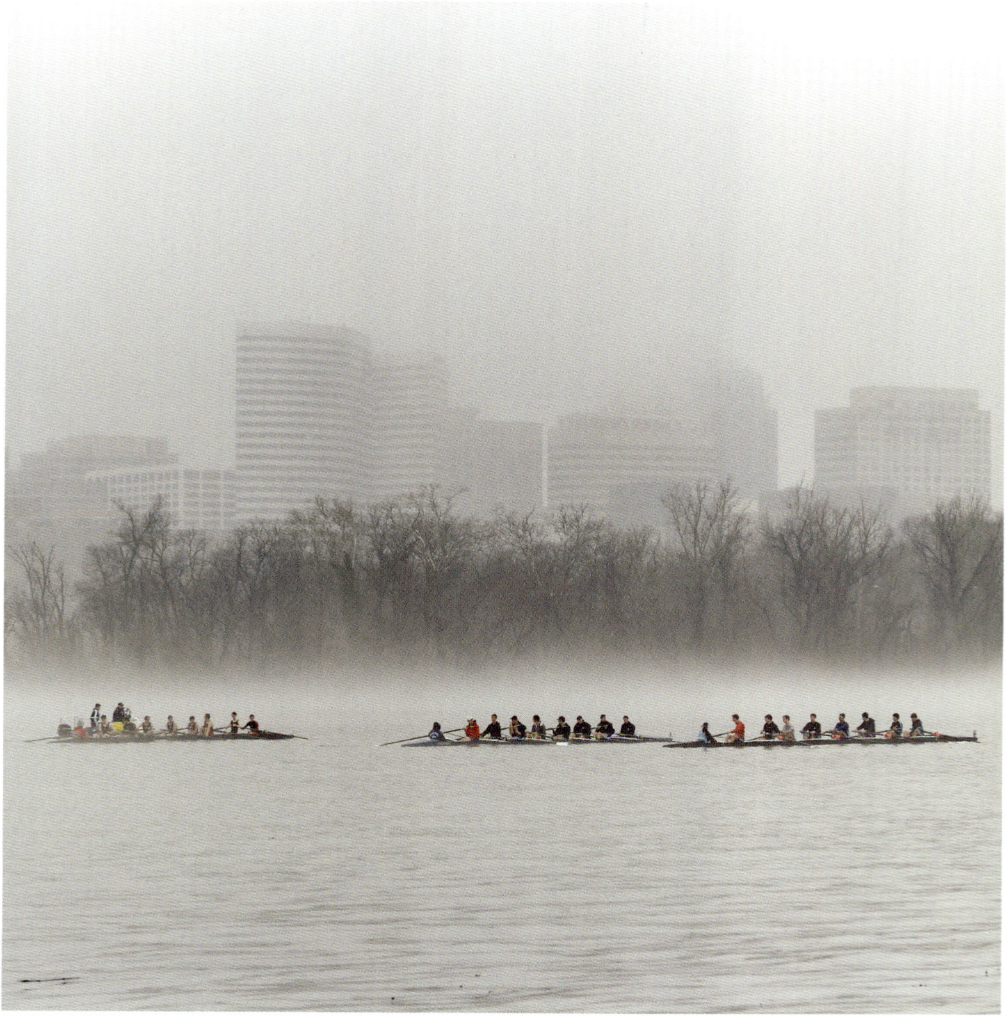

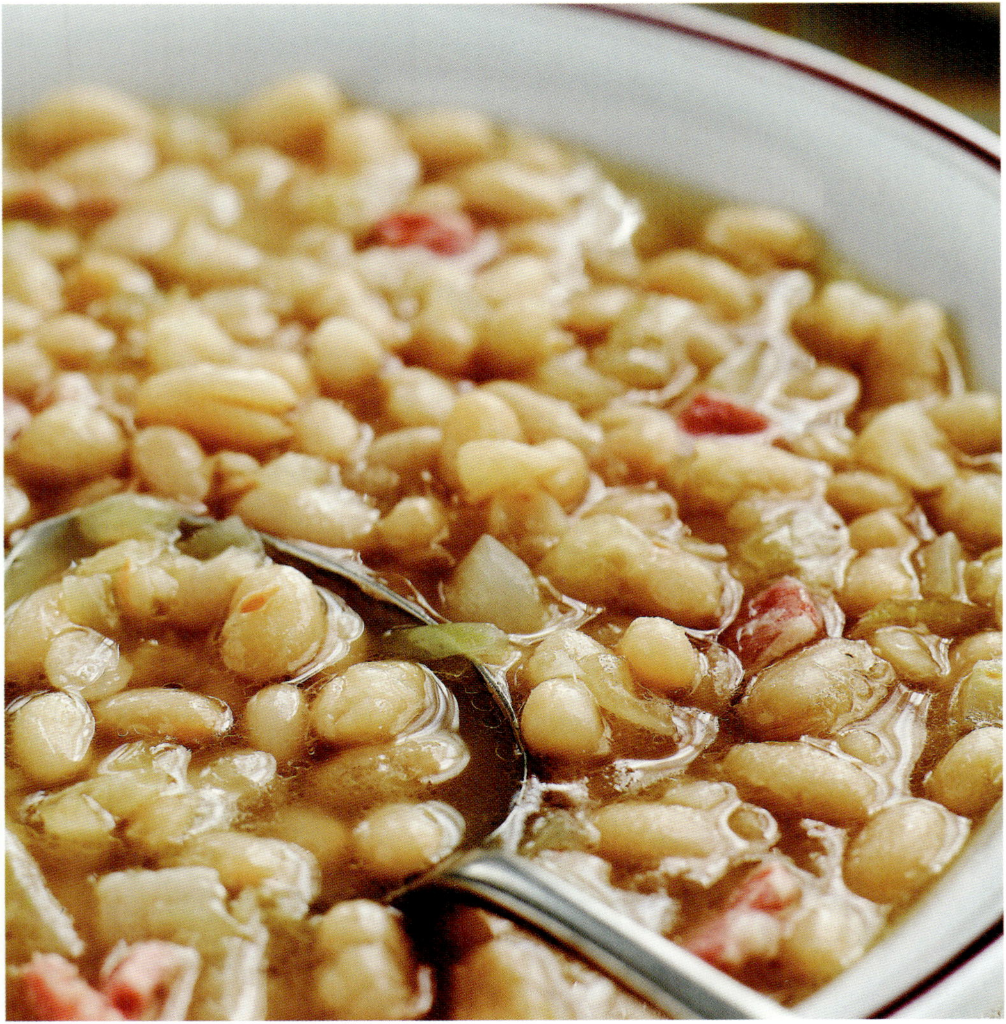

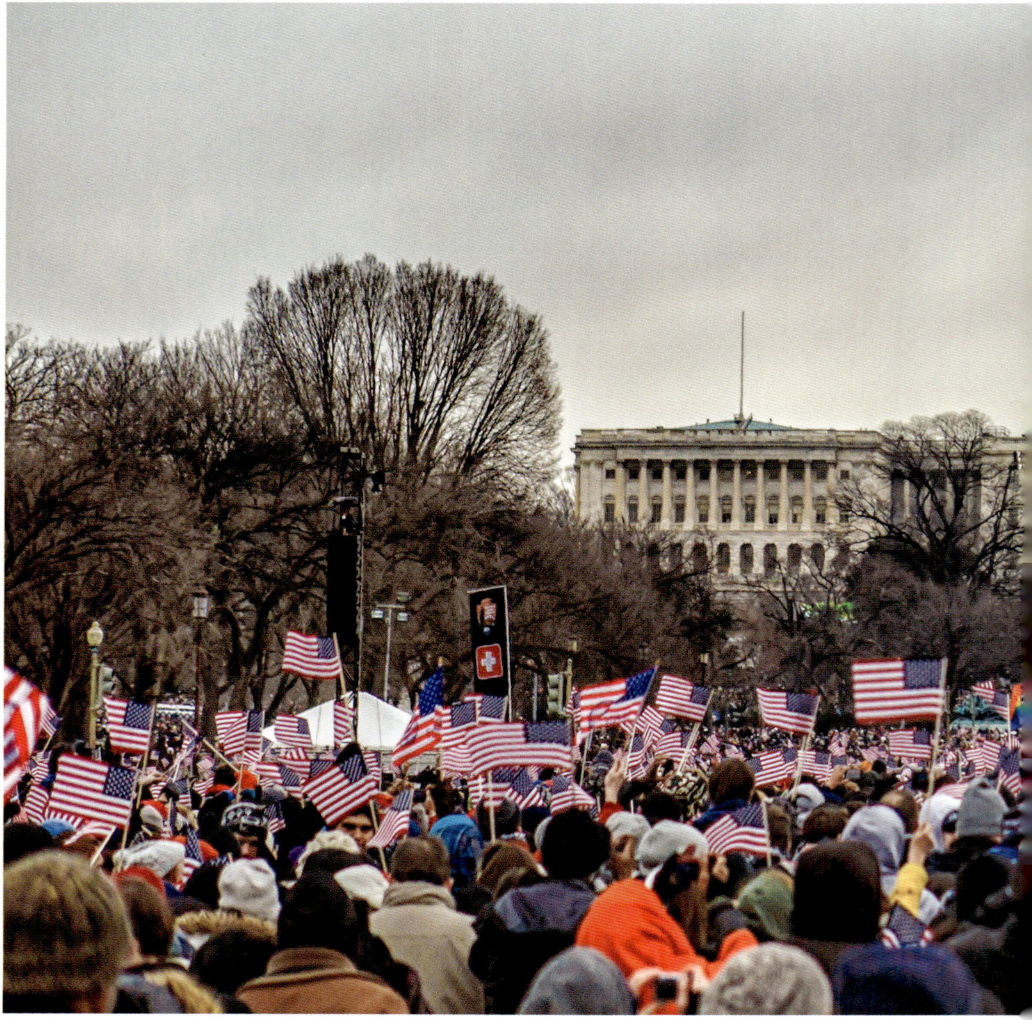

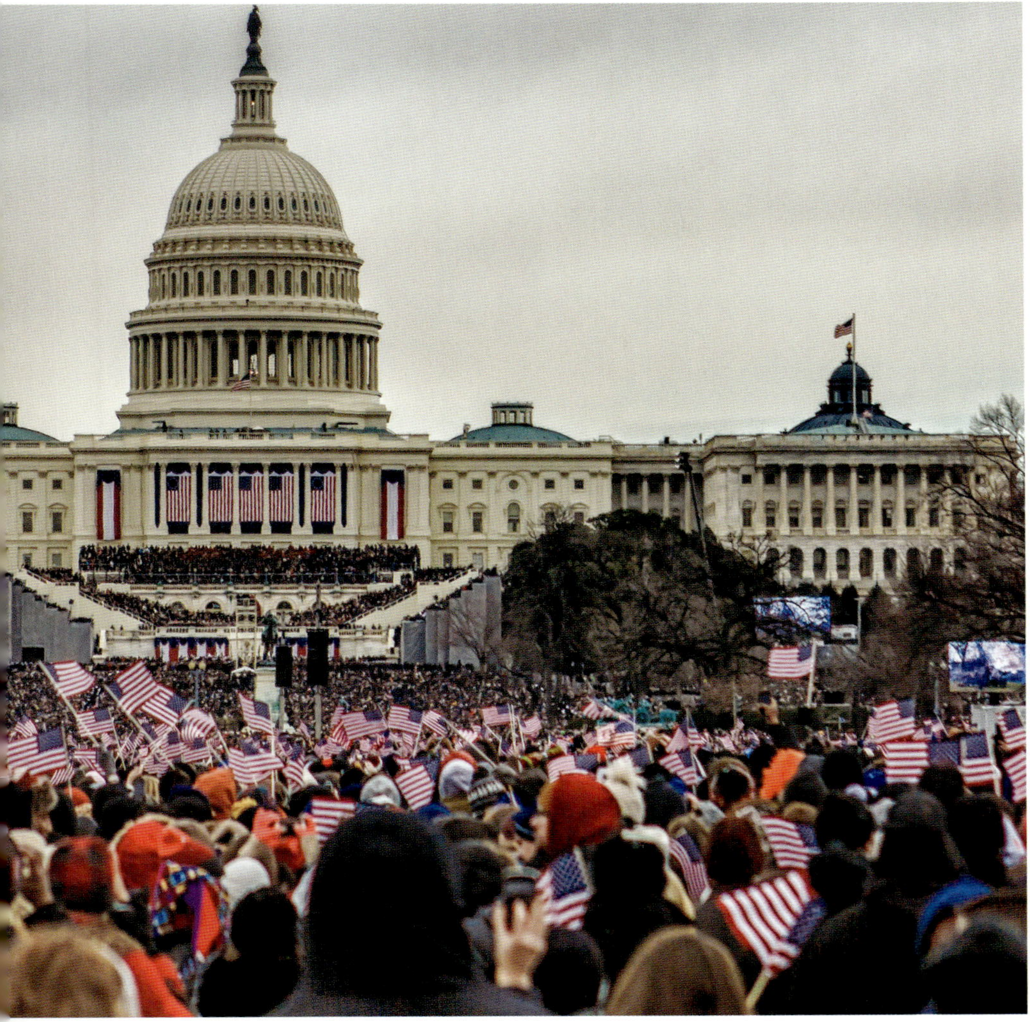

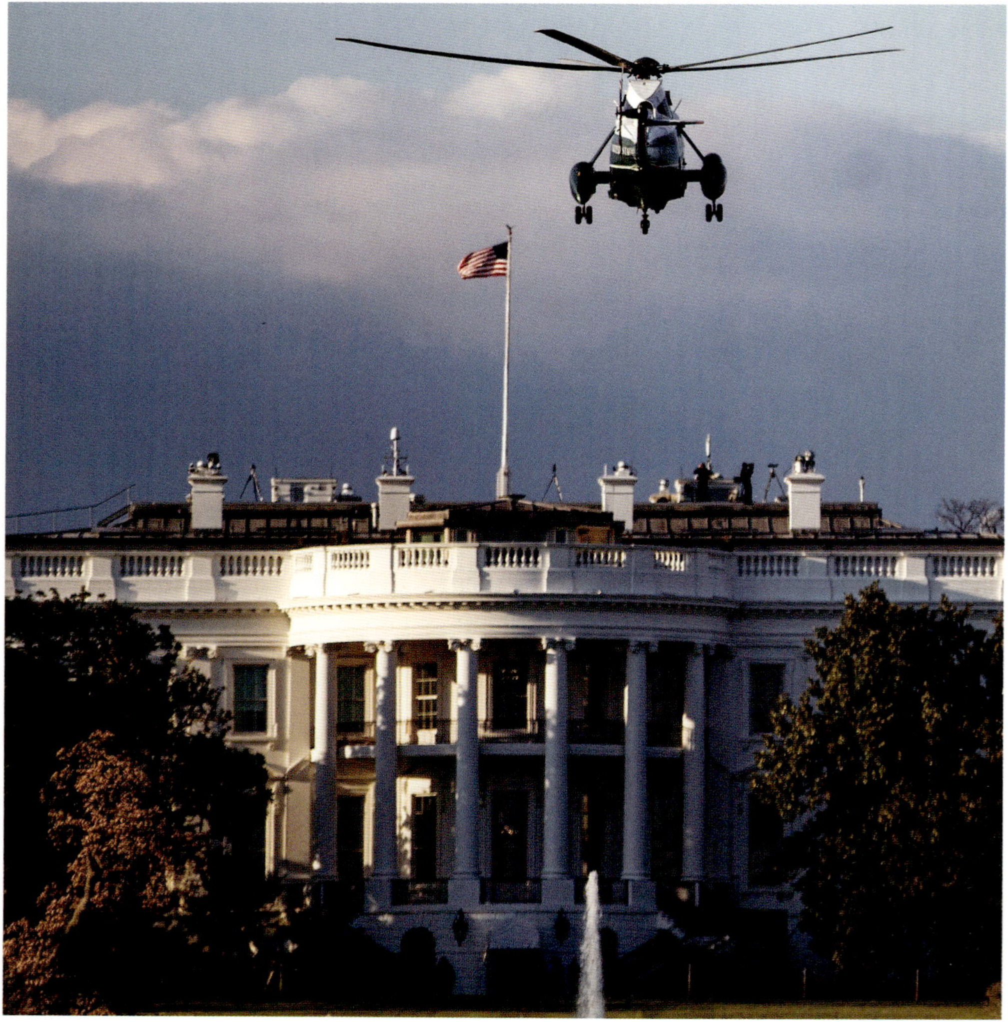

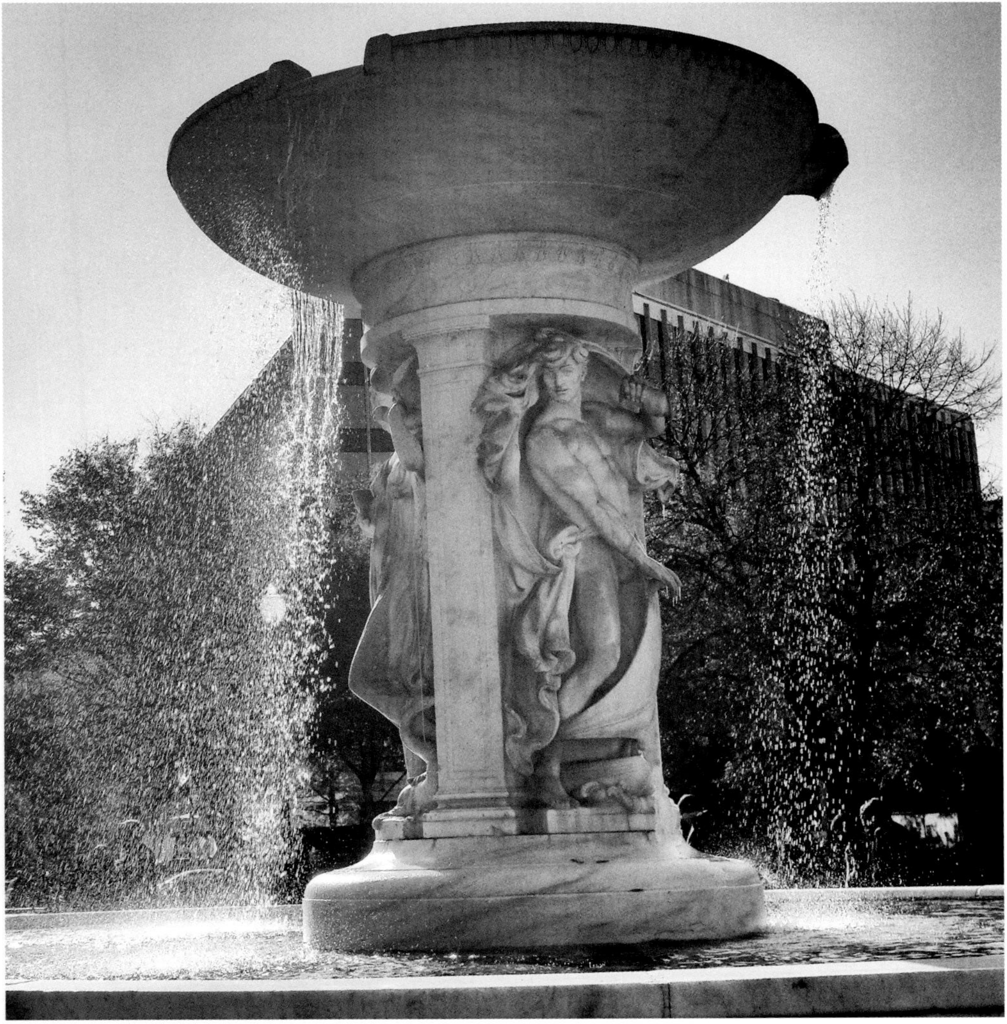

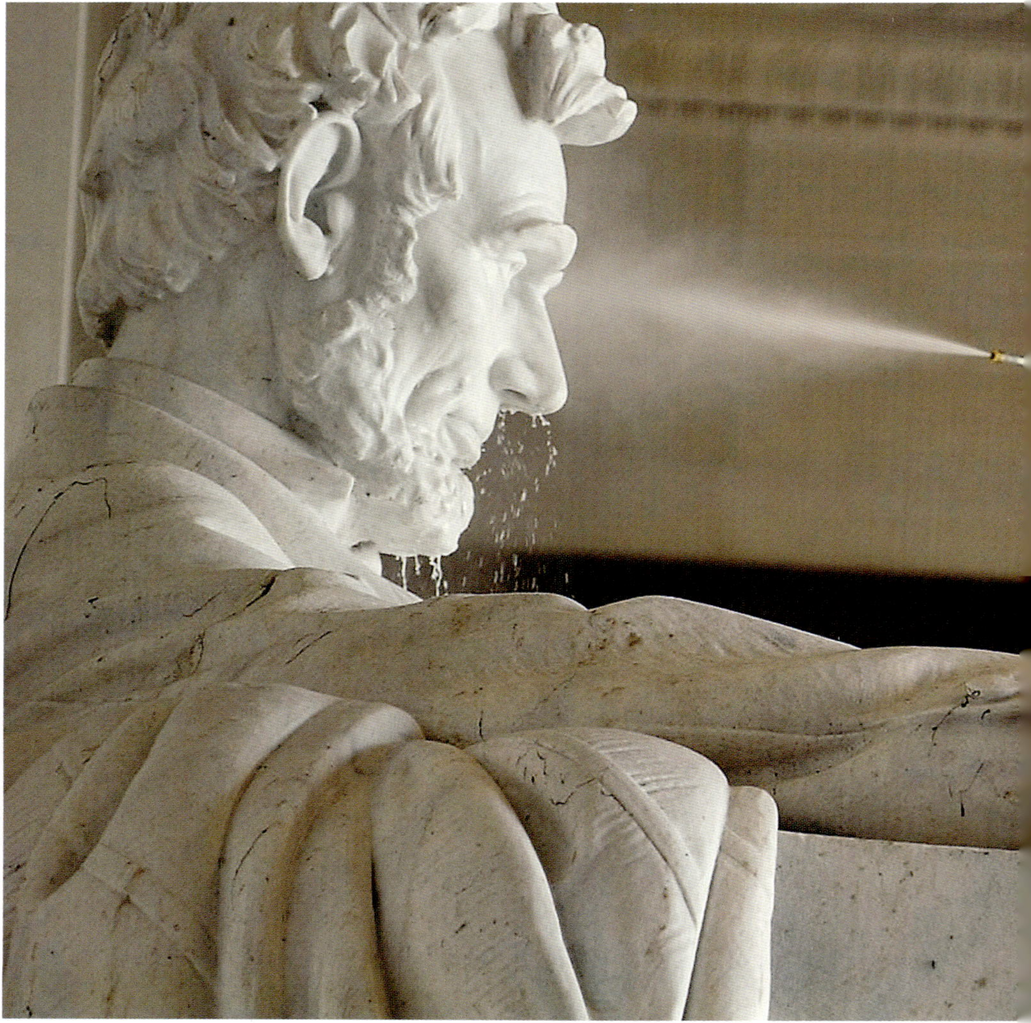

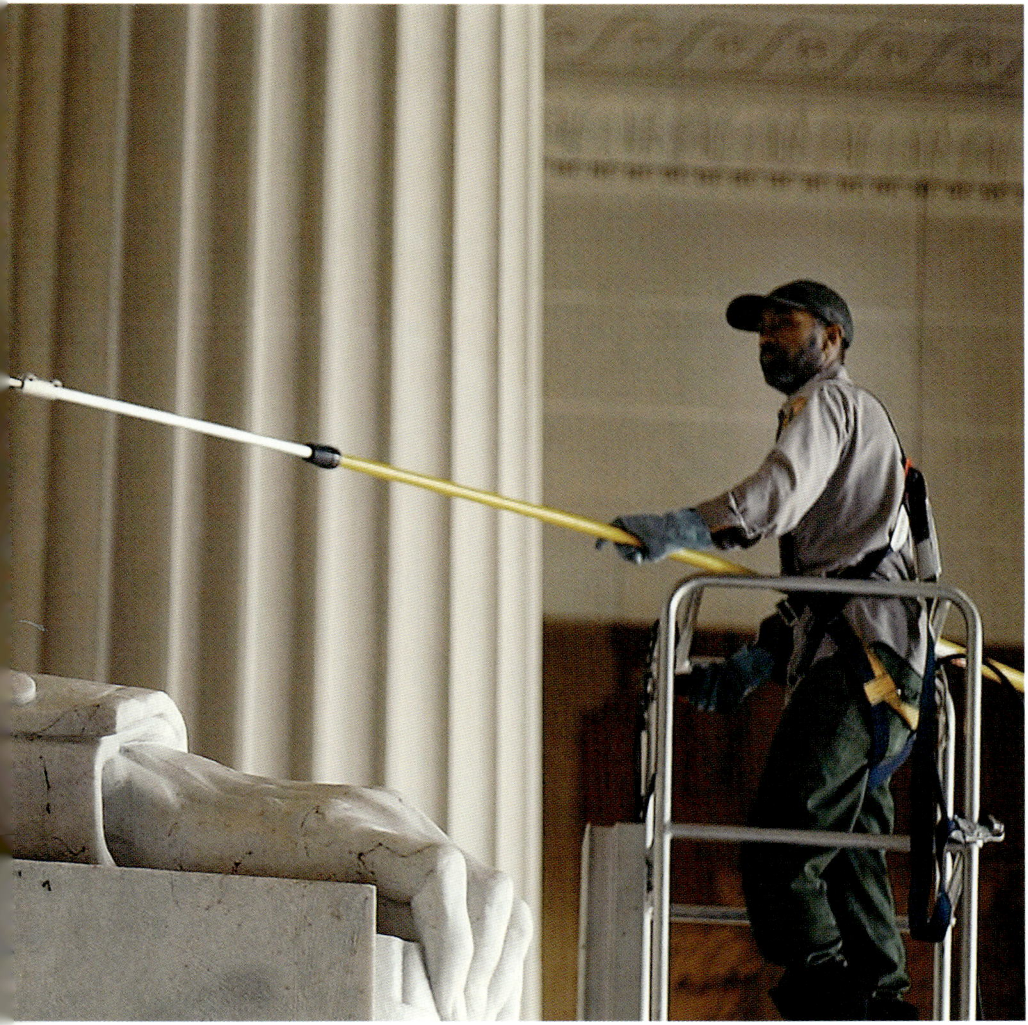

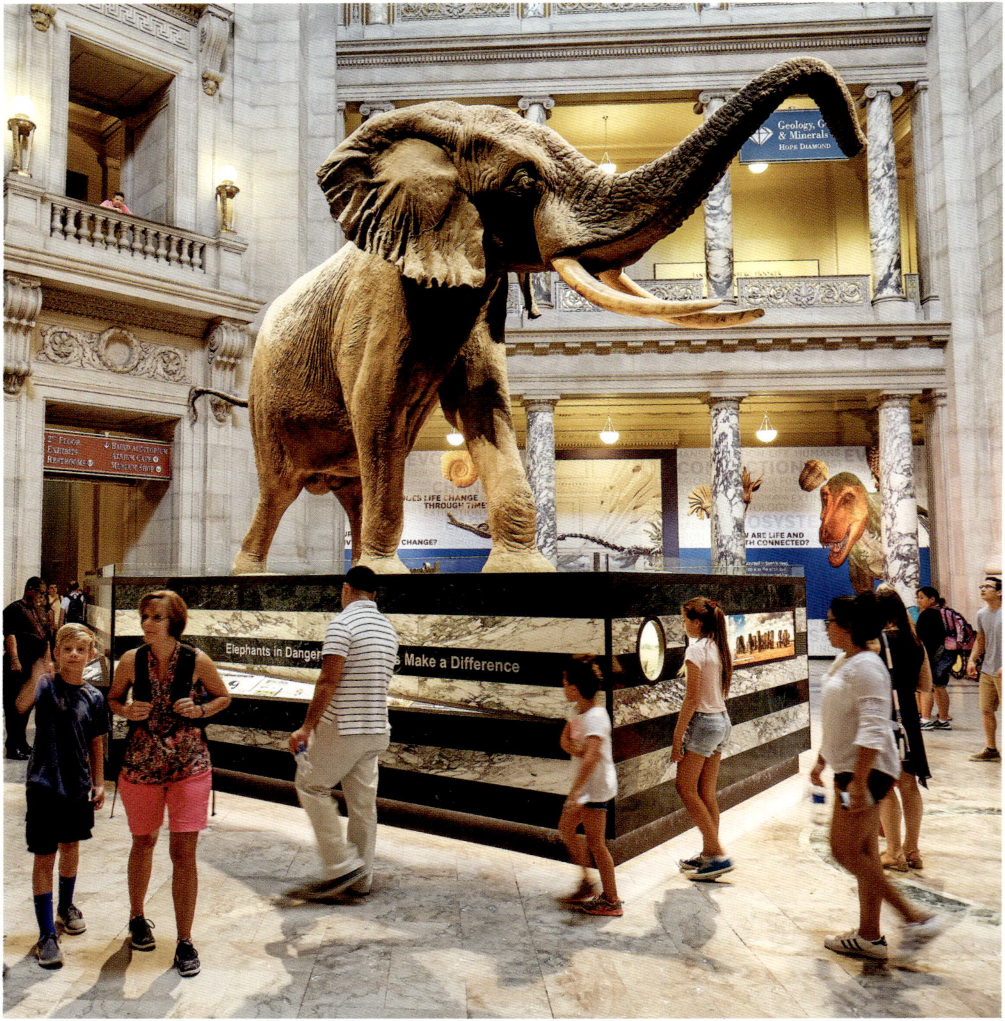

Geology,
& Minerals
HOPE DIAMOND
Elephants in Danger
Make a Difference

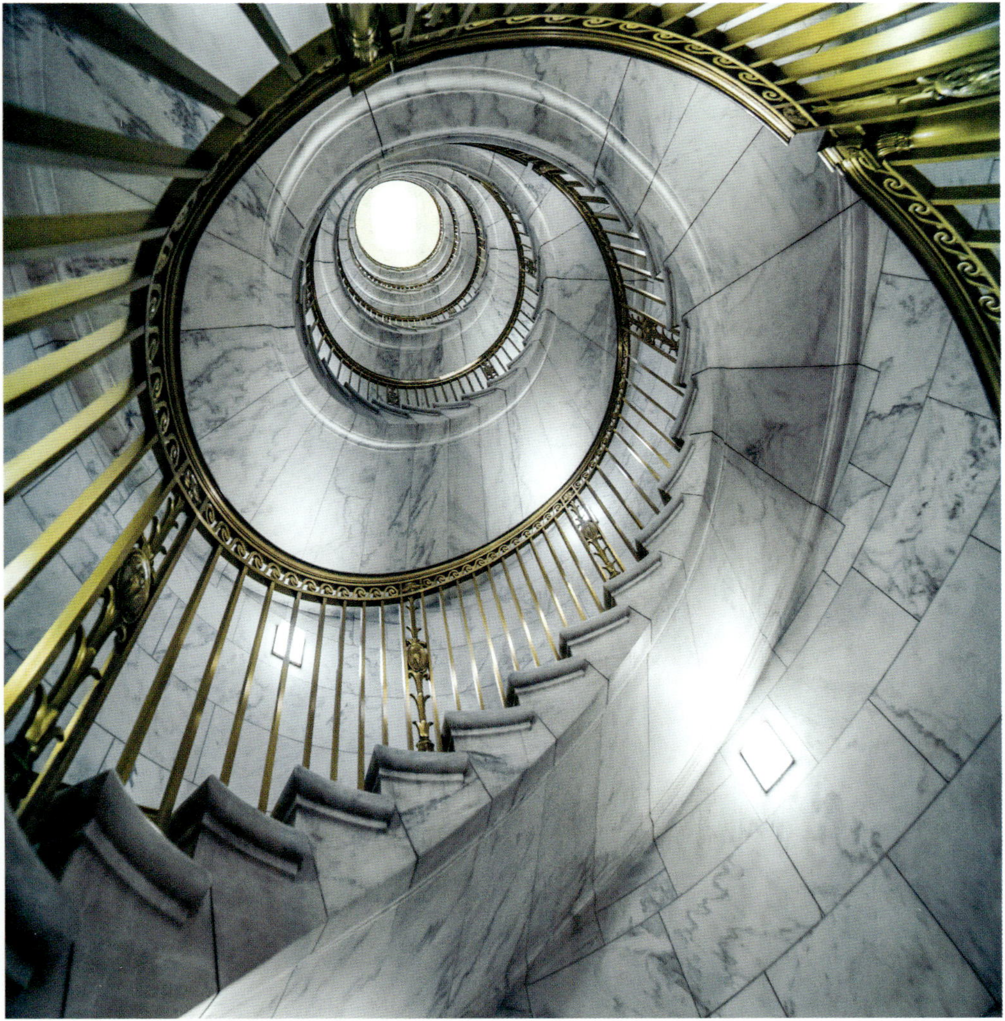

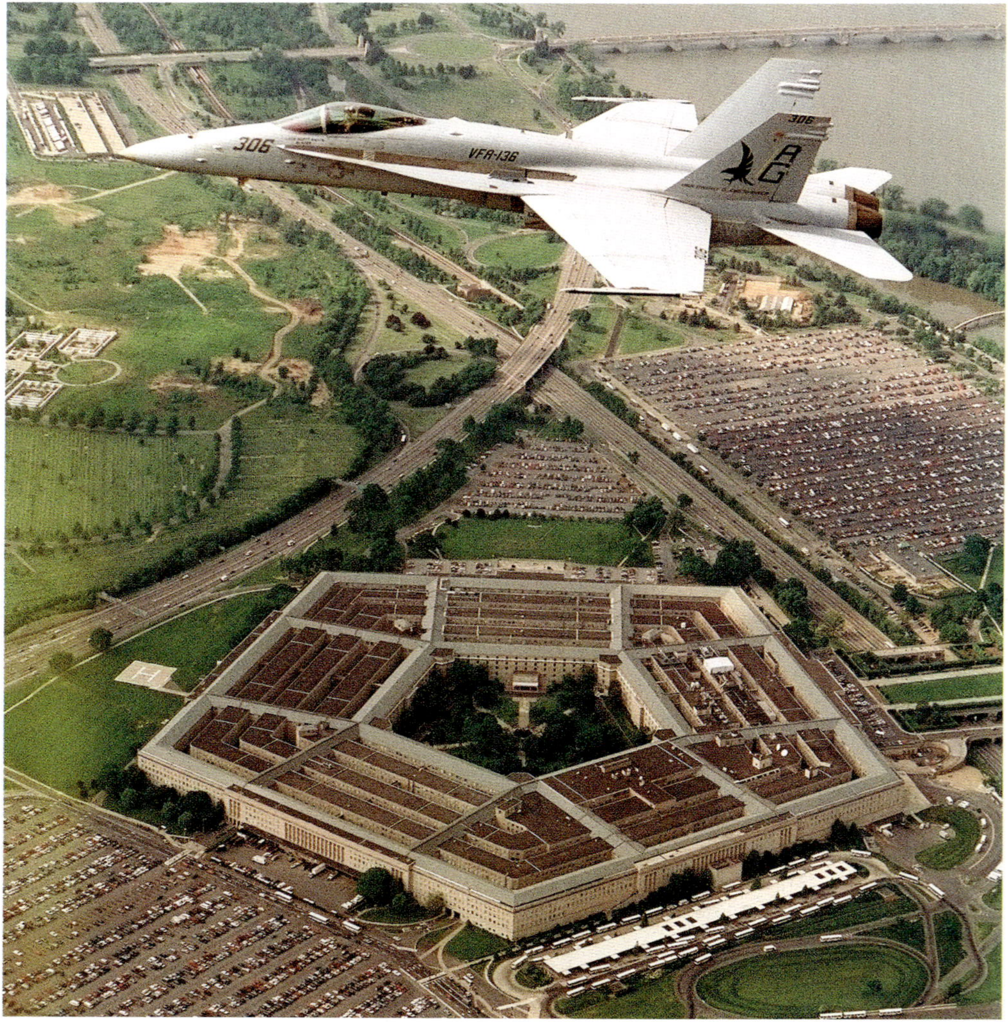
306
VFA-136
306
AG

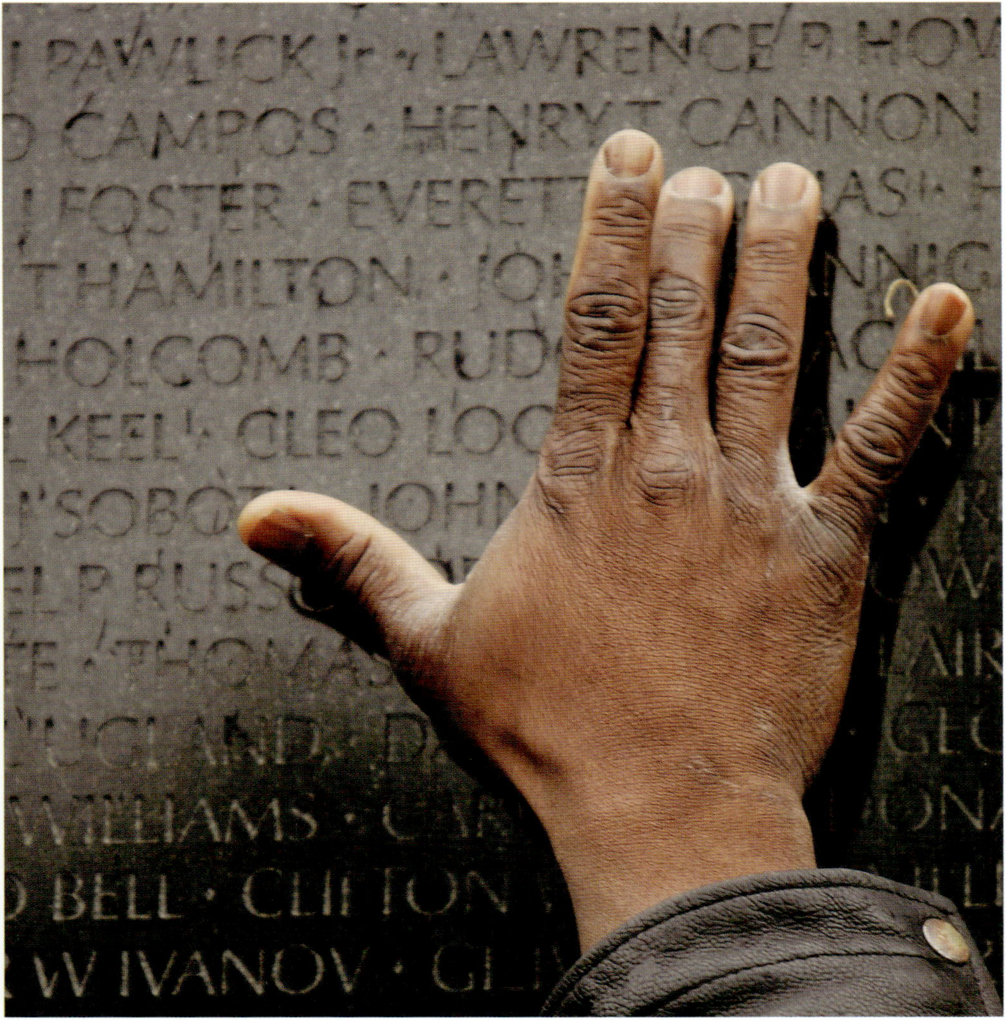
PAWLICK Jr · LAWRENCE P
CAMPOS · HENRY T CANNON
FOSTER · EVERETT
HAMILTON
HOLCOMB
KEEL · CLEO
WILLIAMS
BELL · CLIFTON
W IVANOV

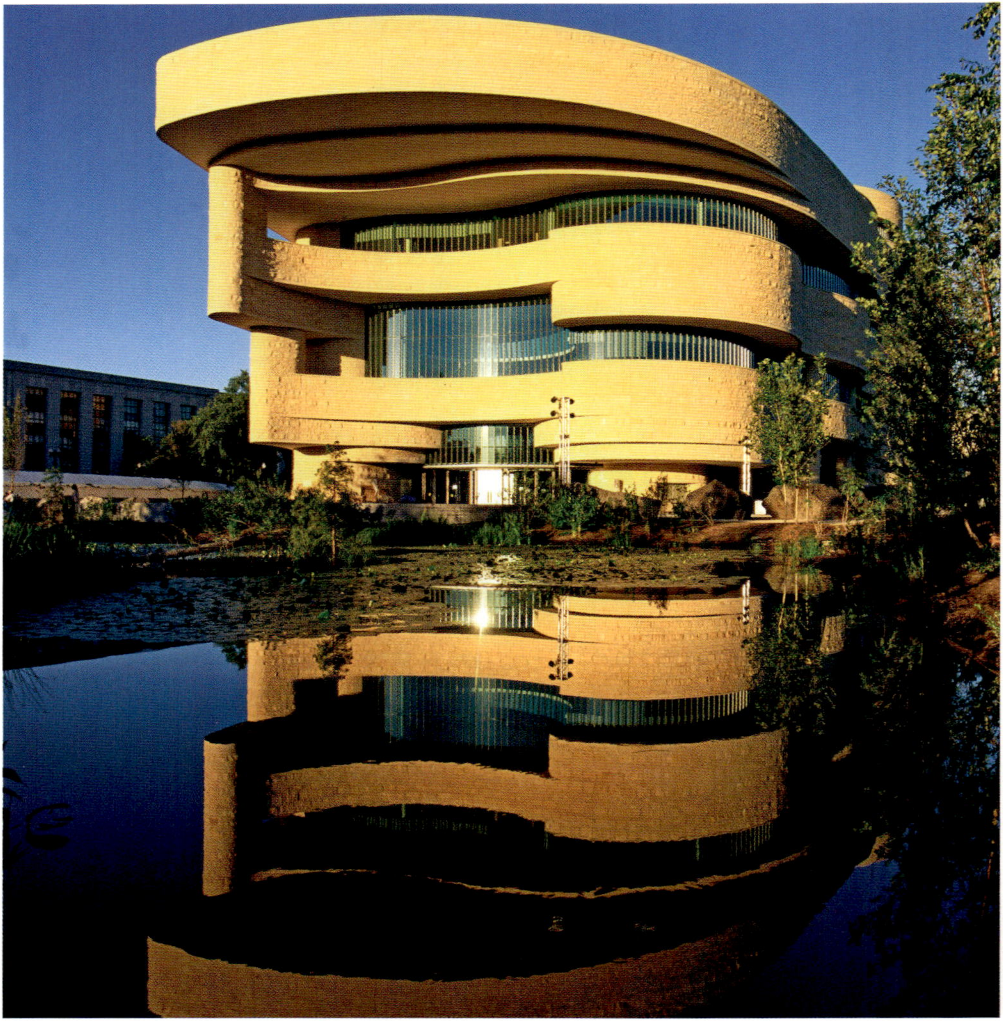

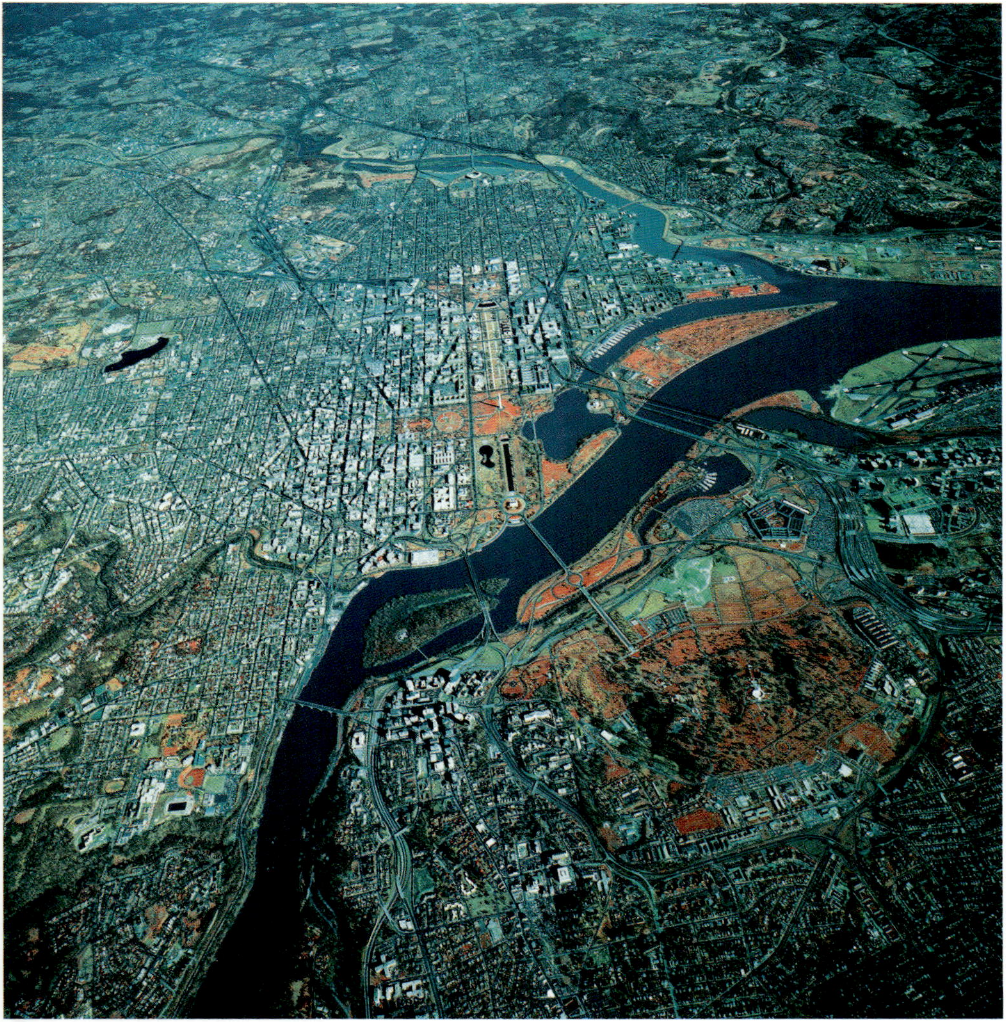

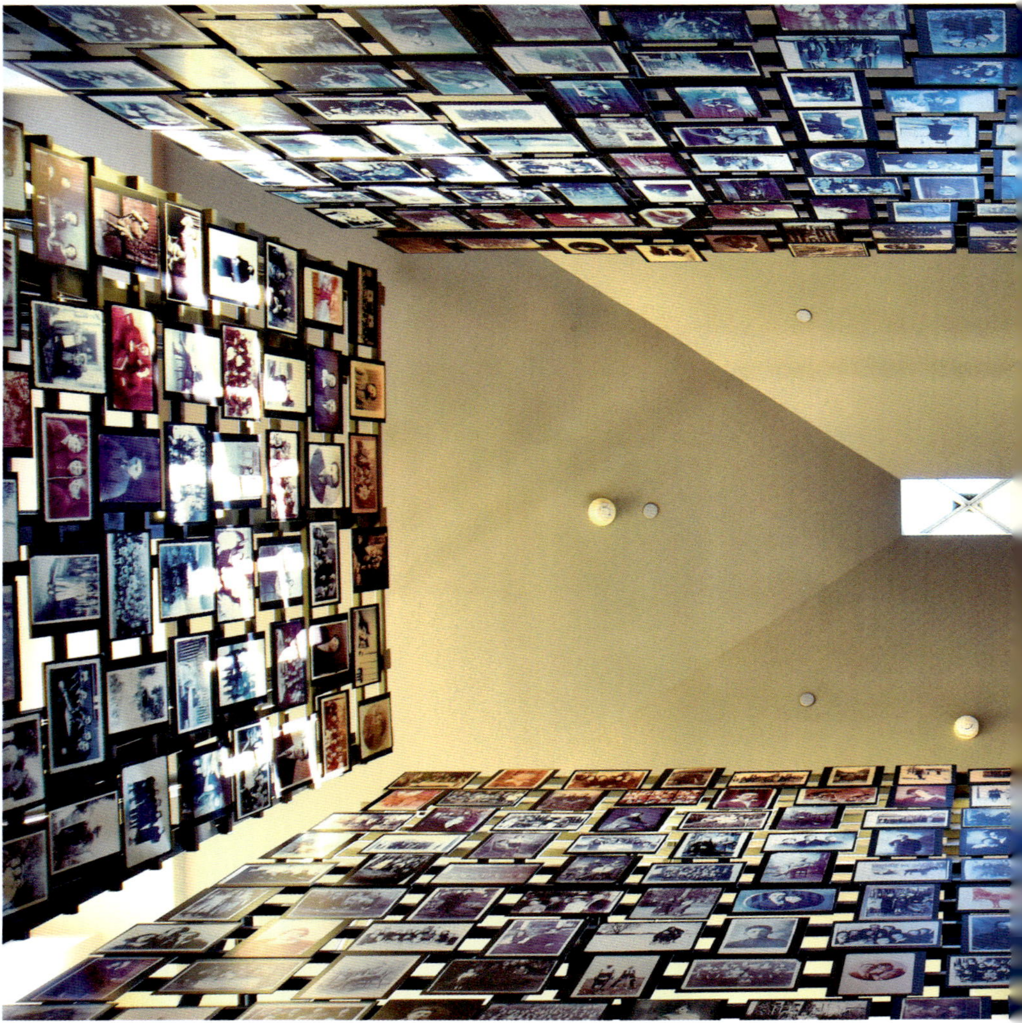

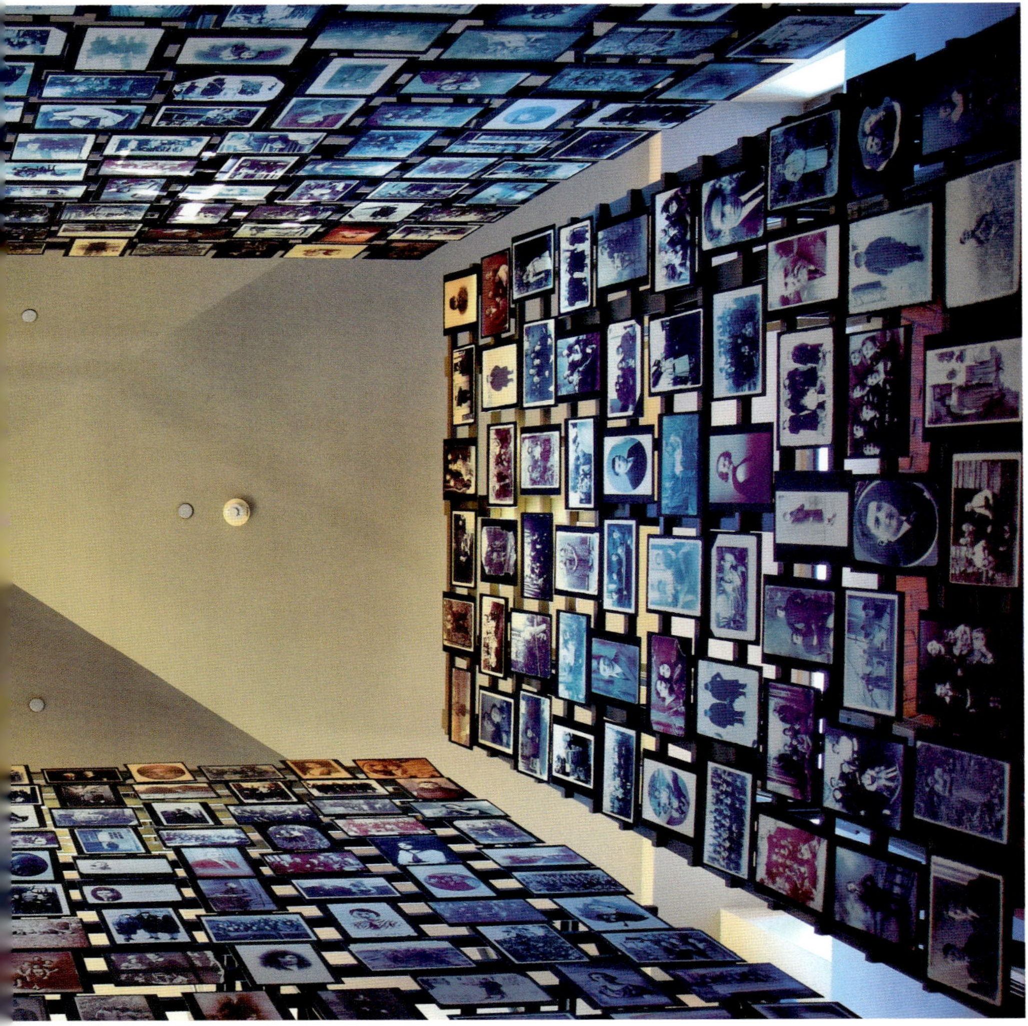

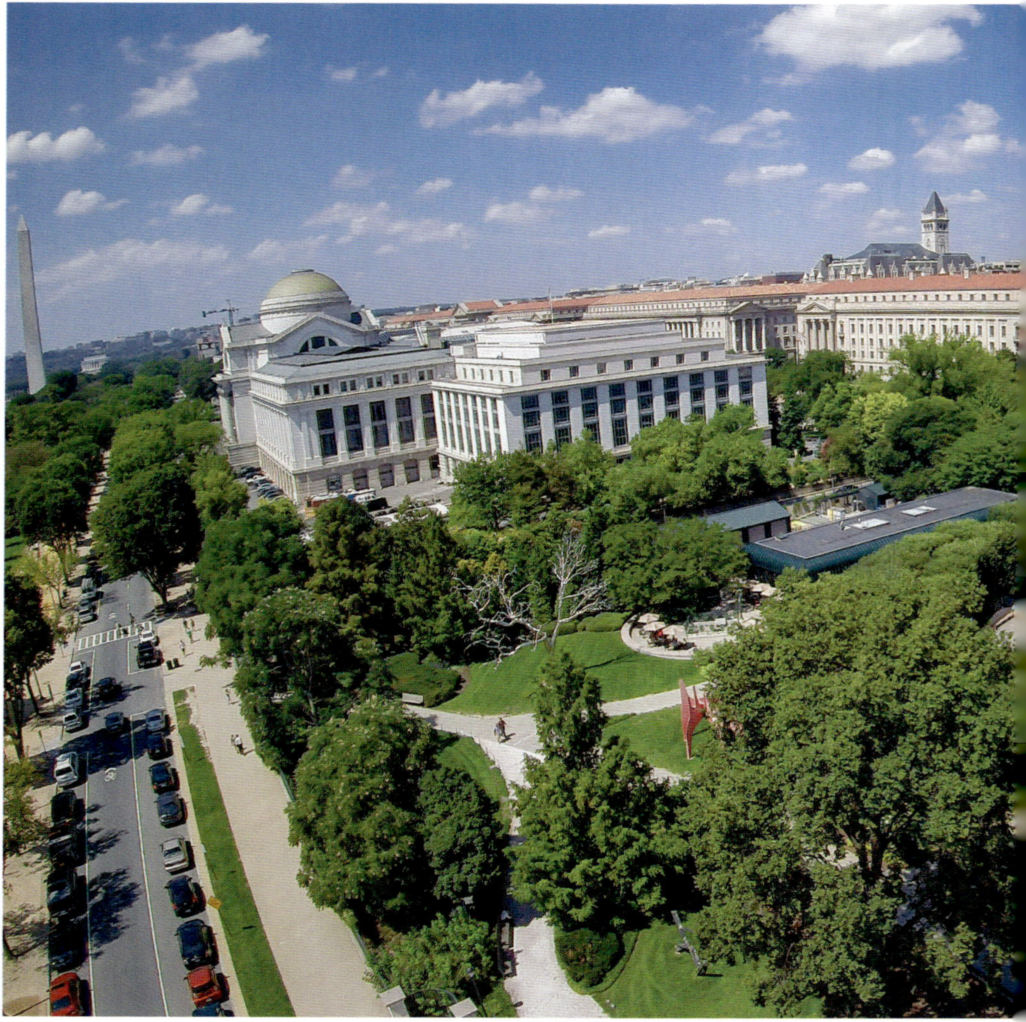

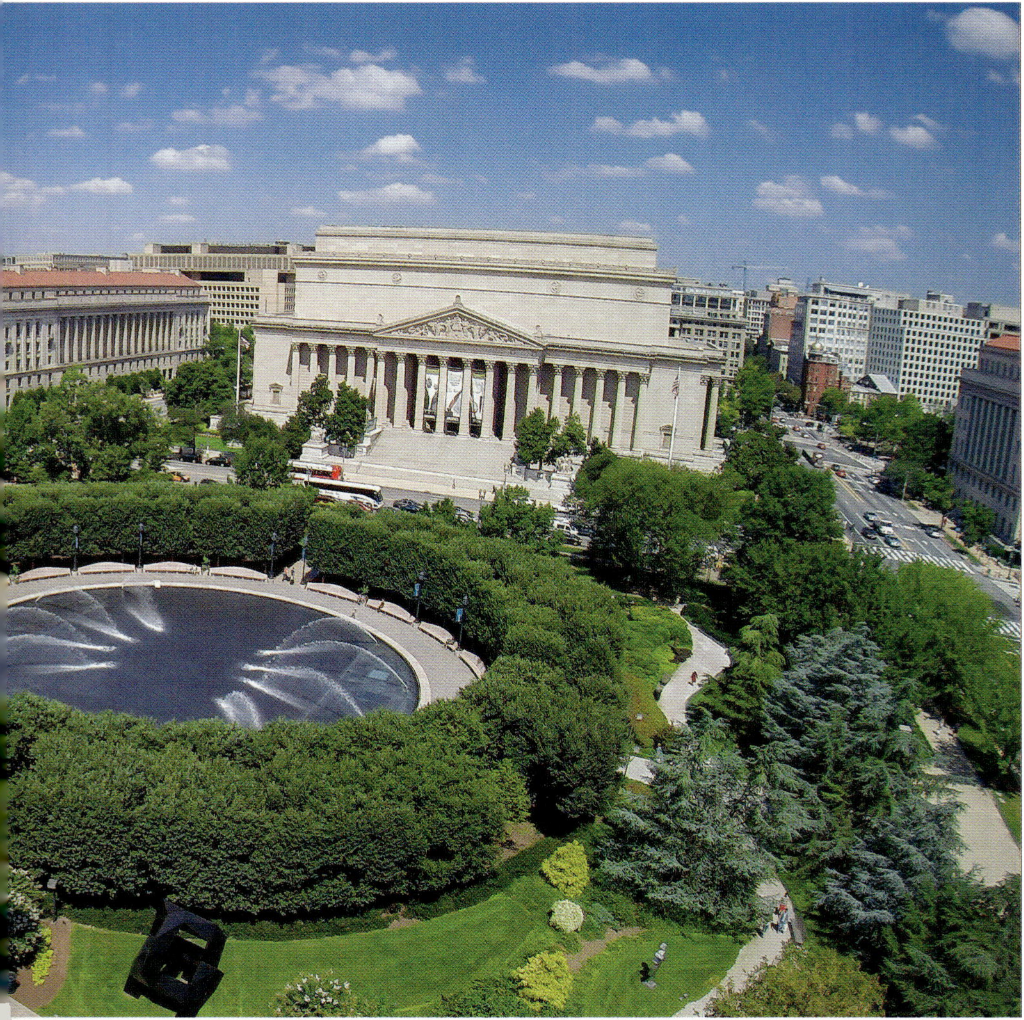

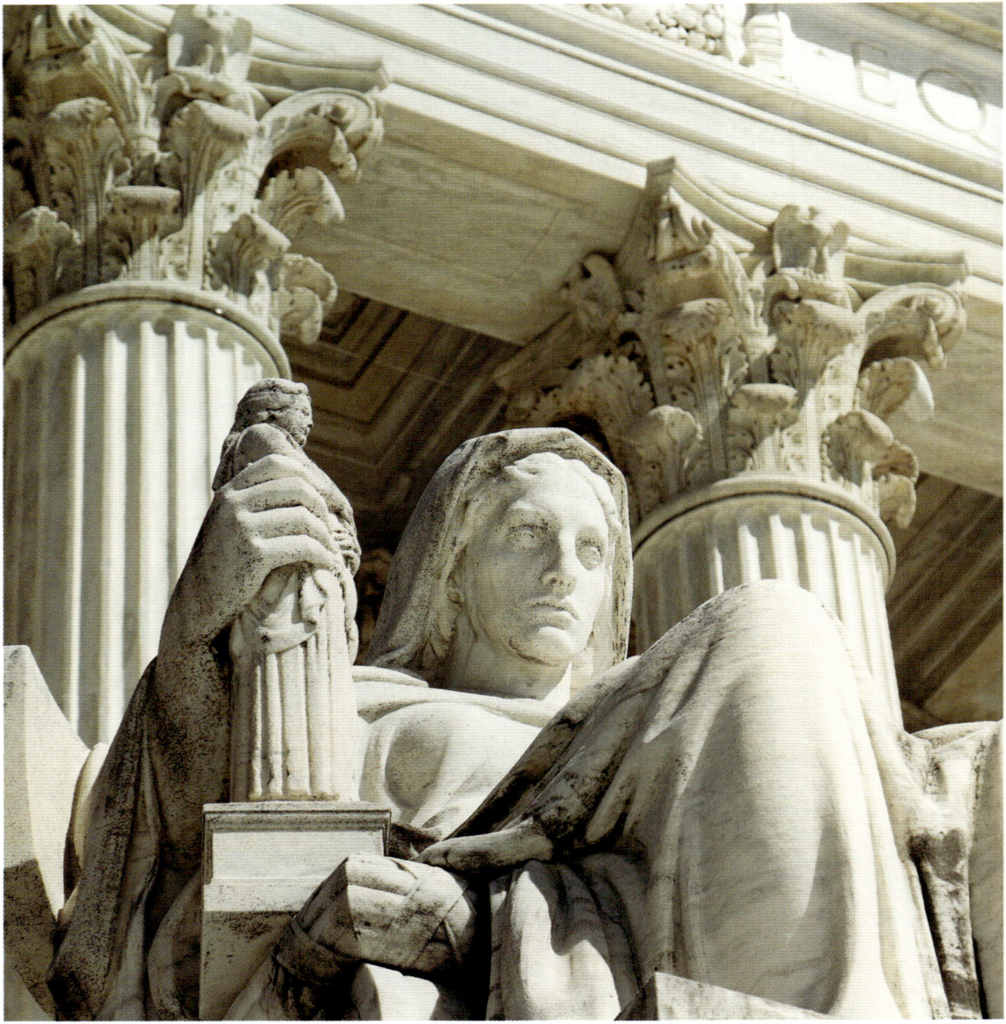

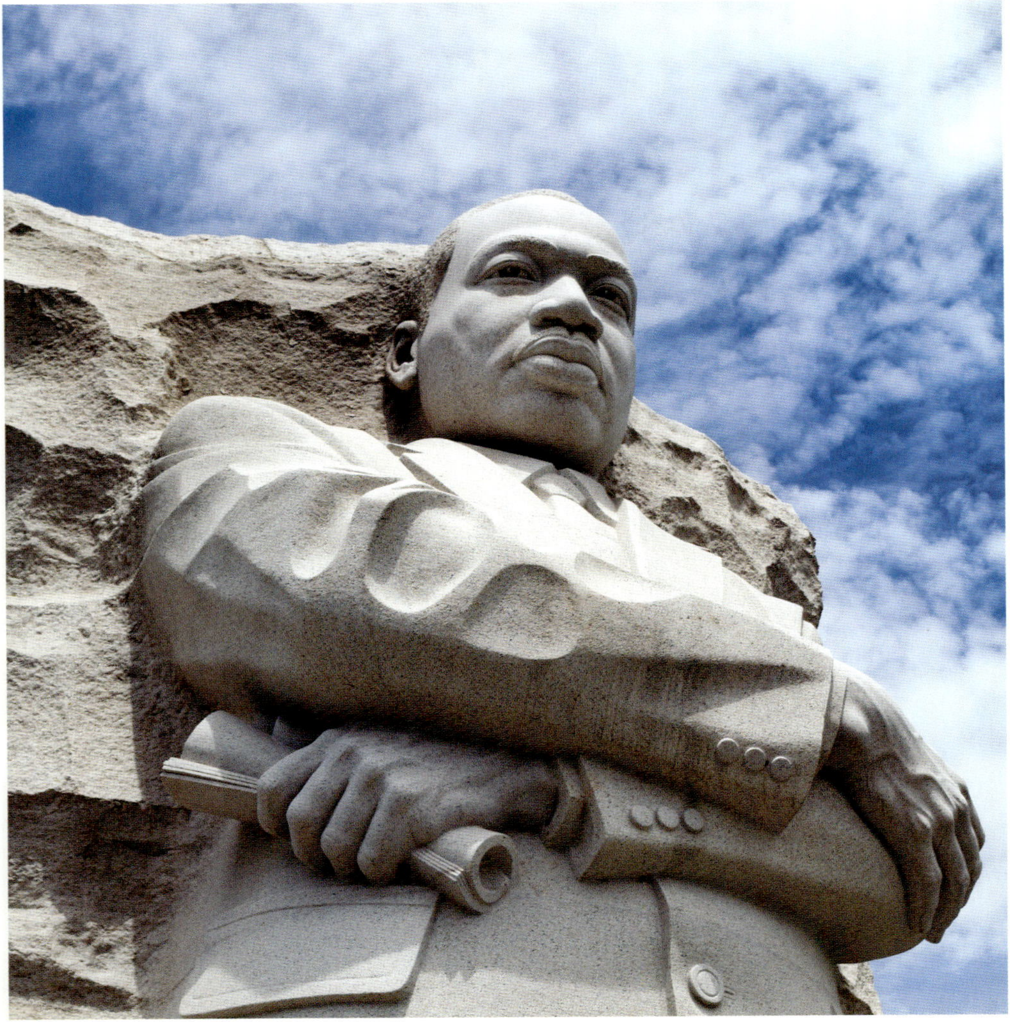

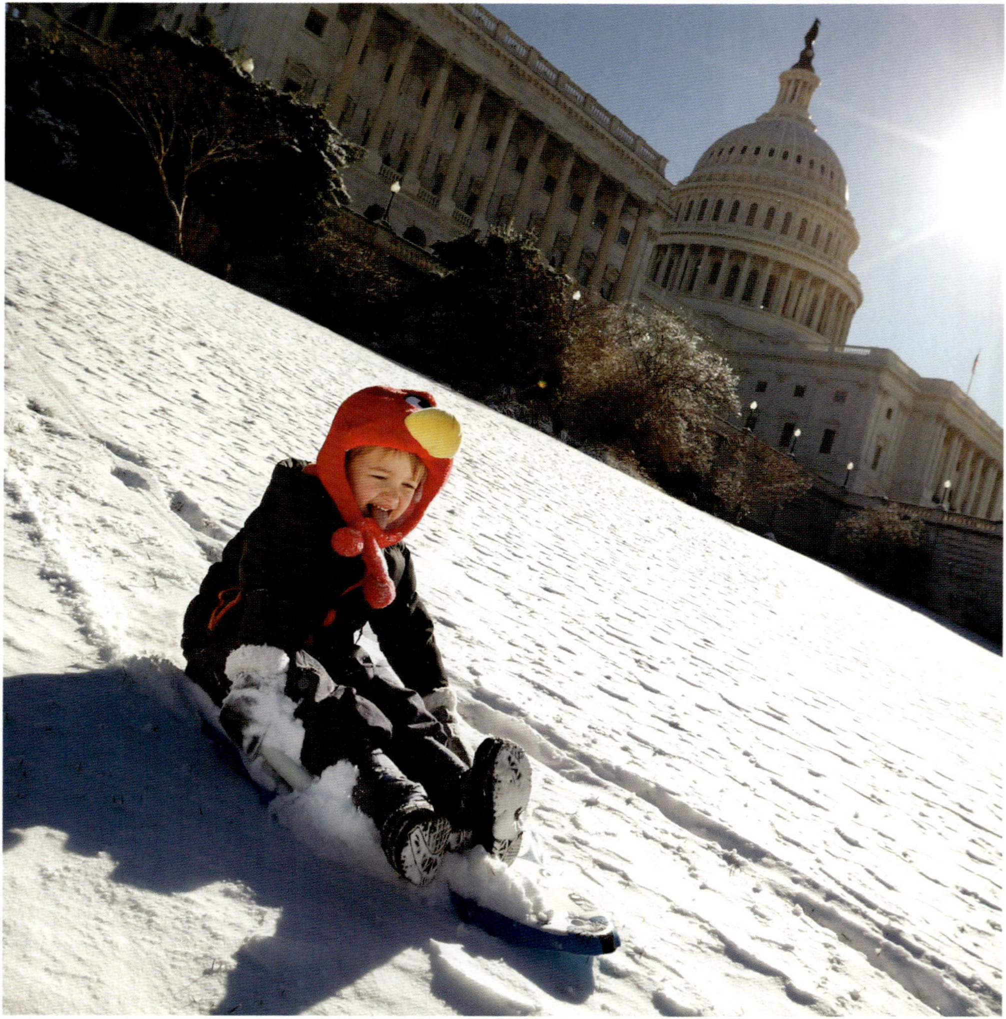

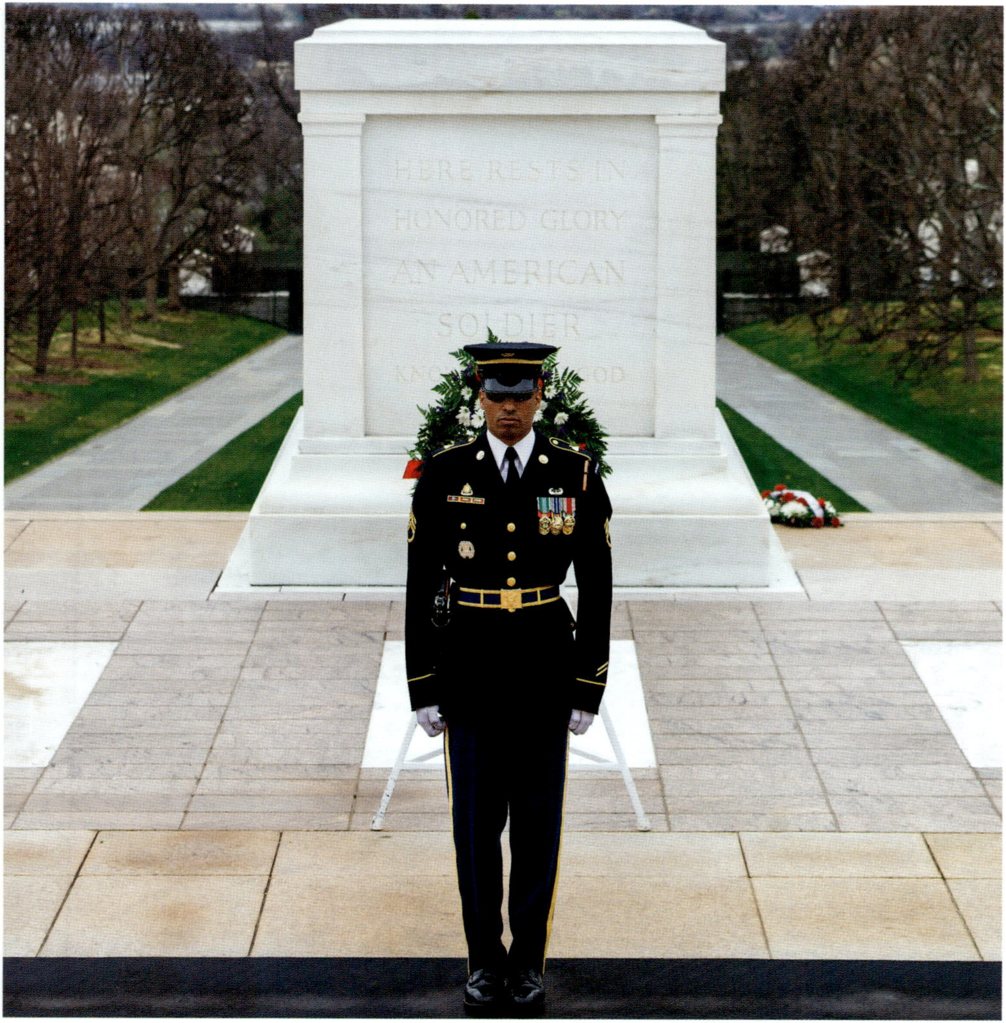
HERE RESTS IN
HONORED GLORY
AN AMERICAN
SOLDIER

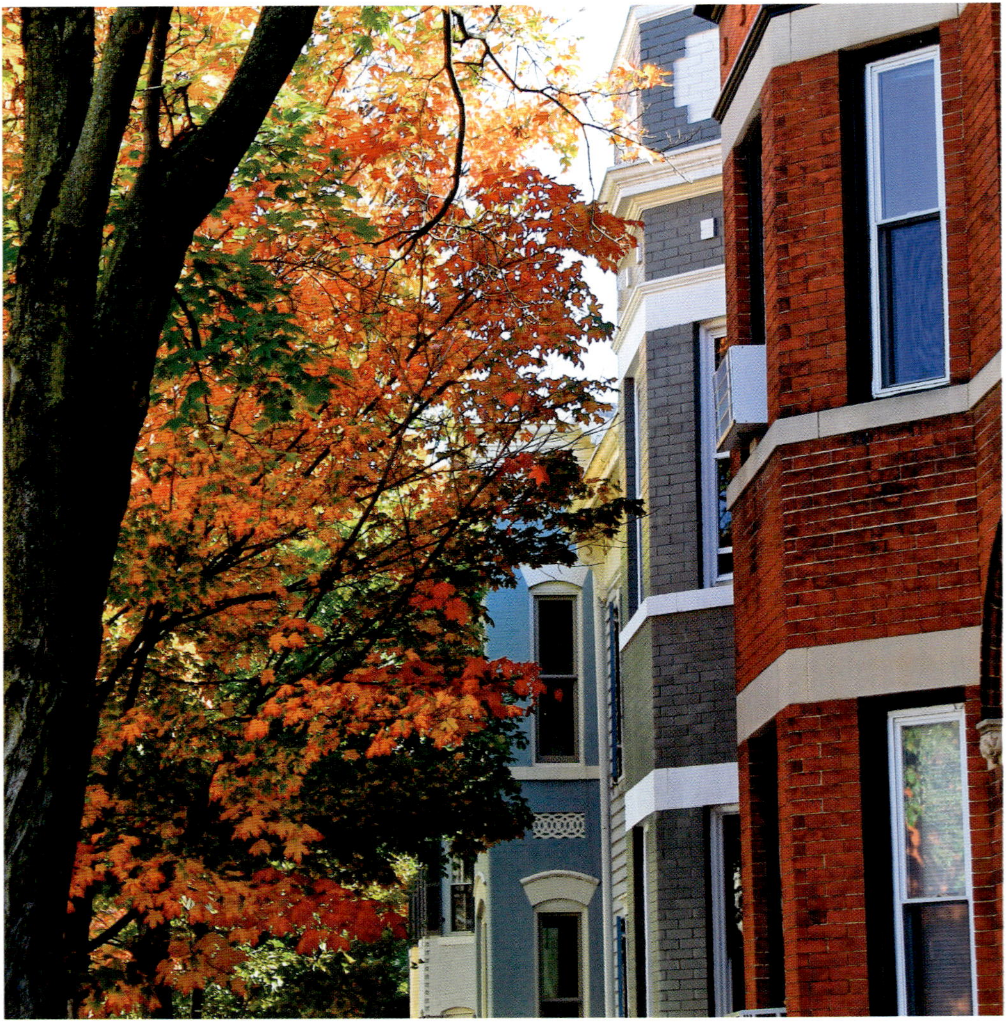

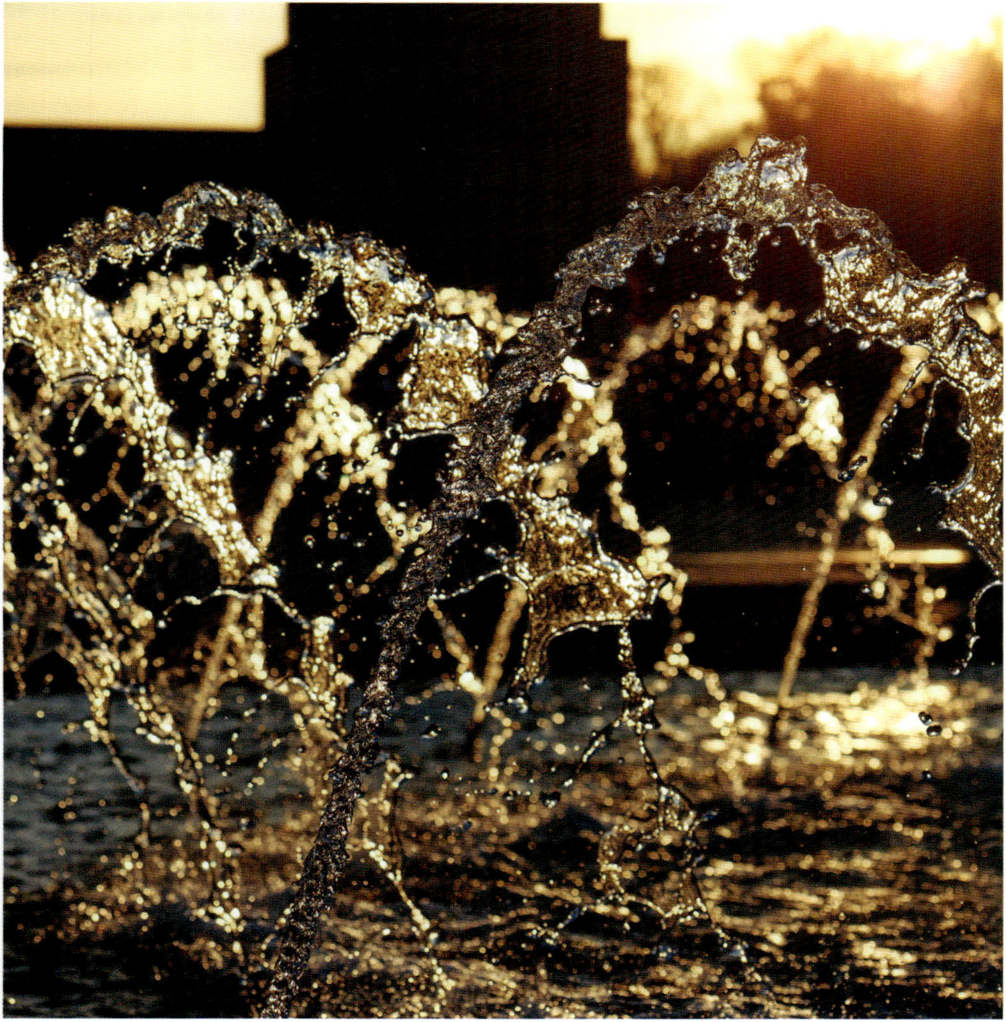

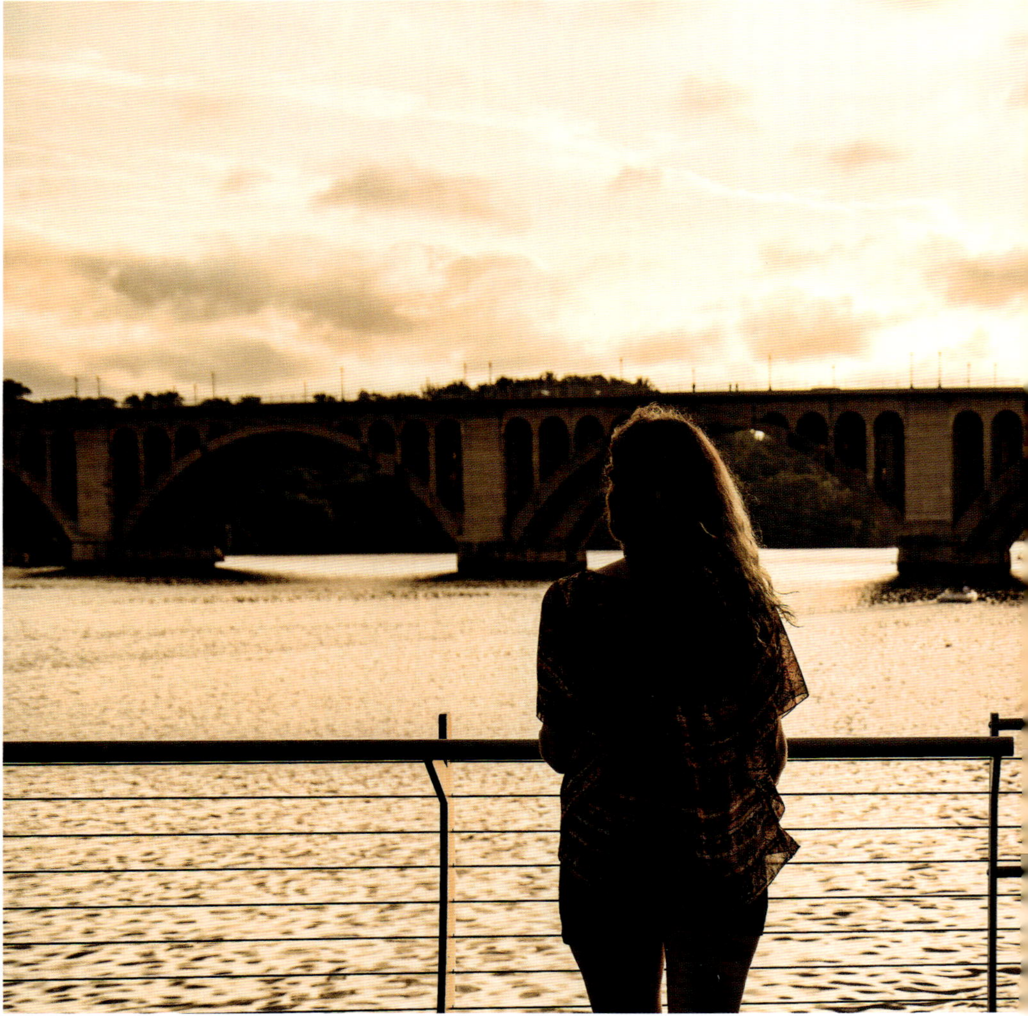

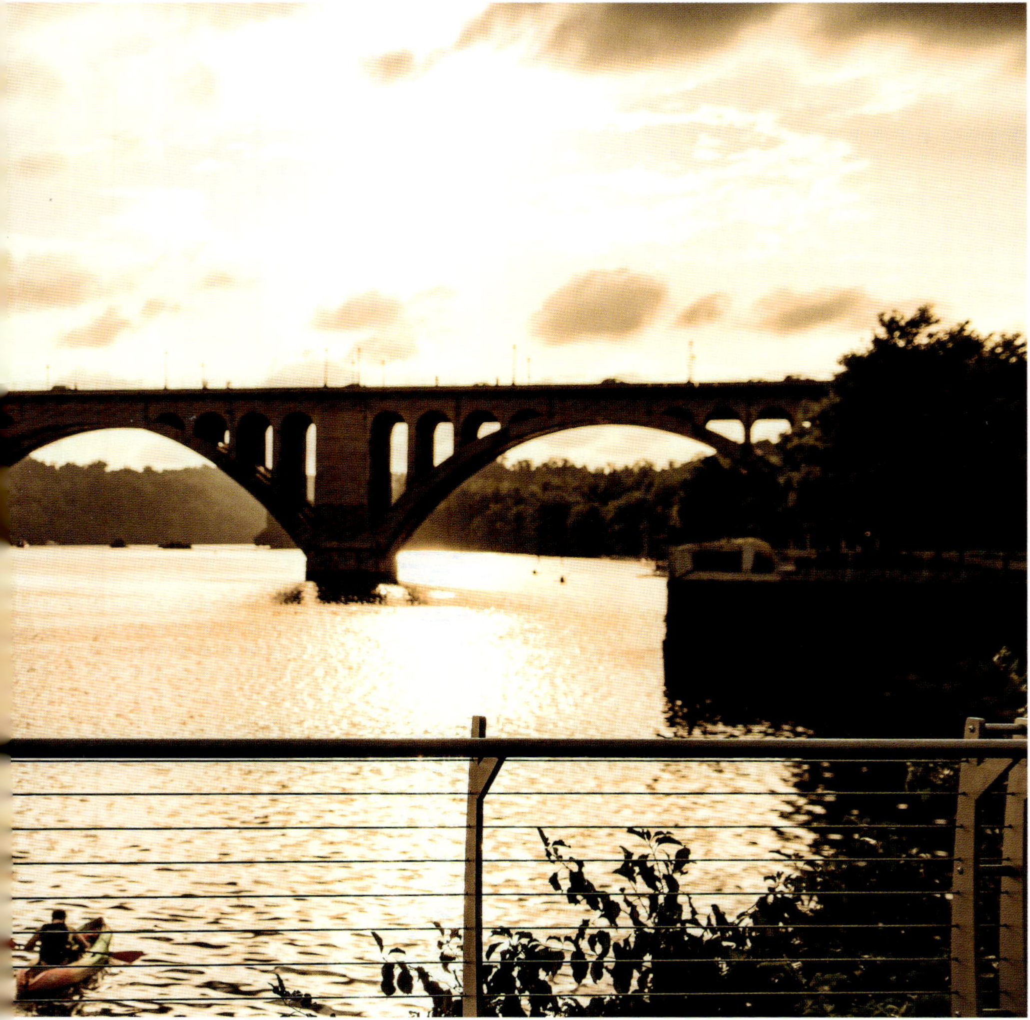

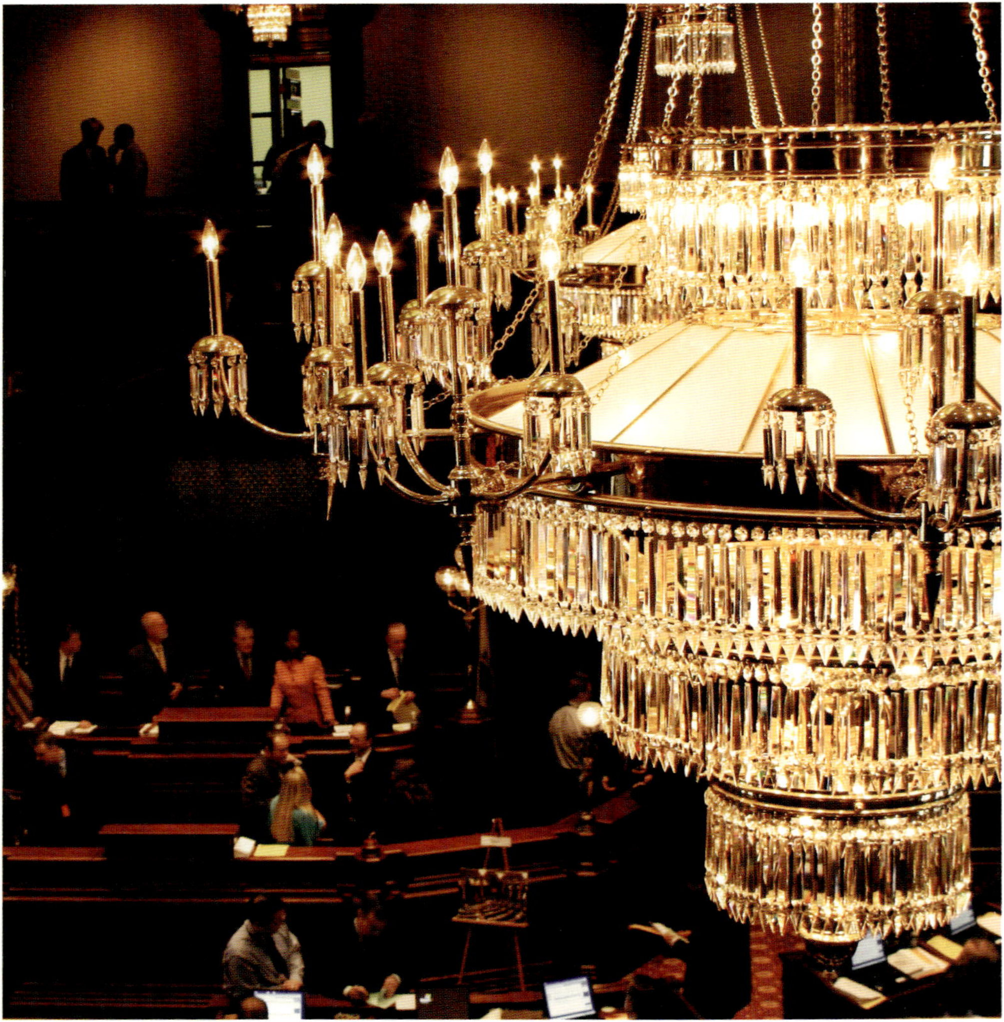

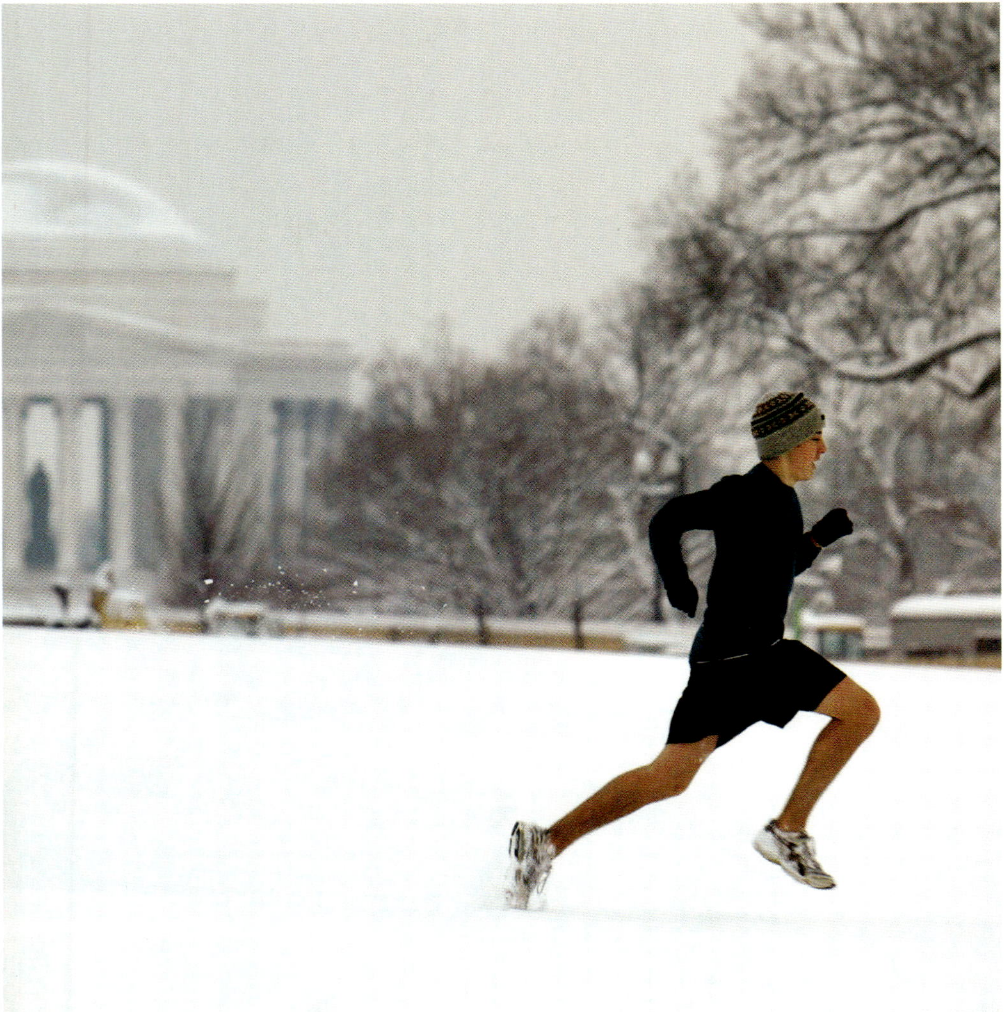

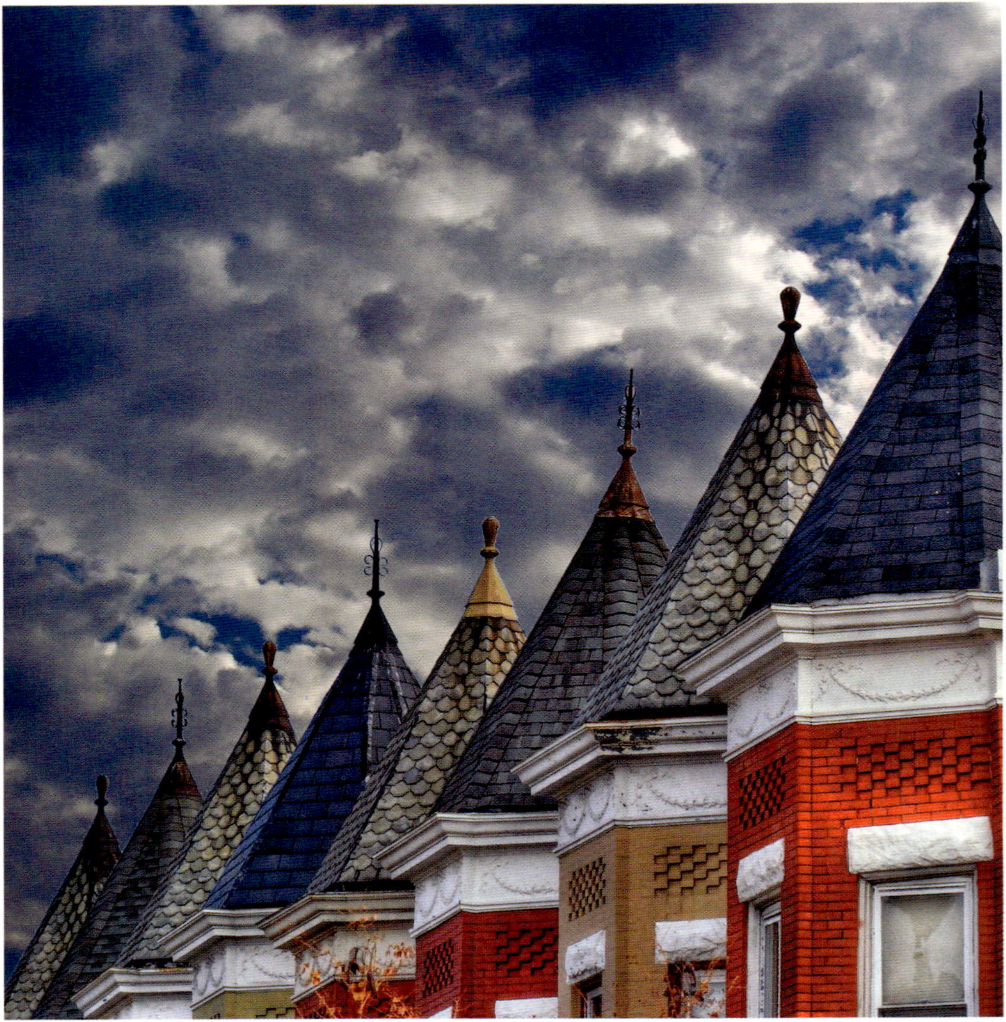

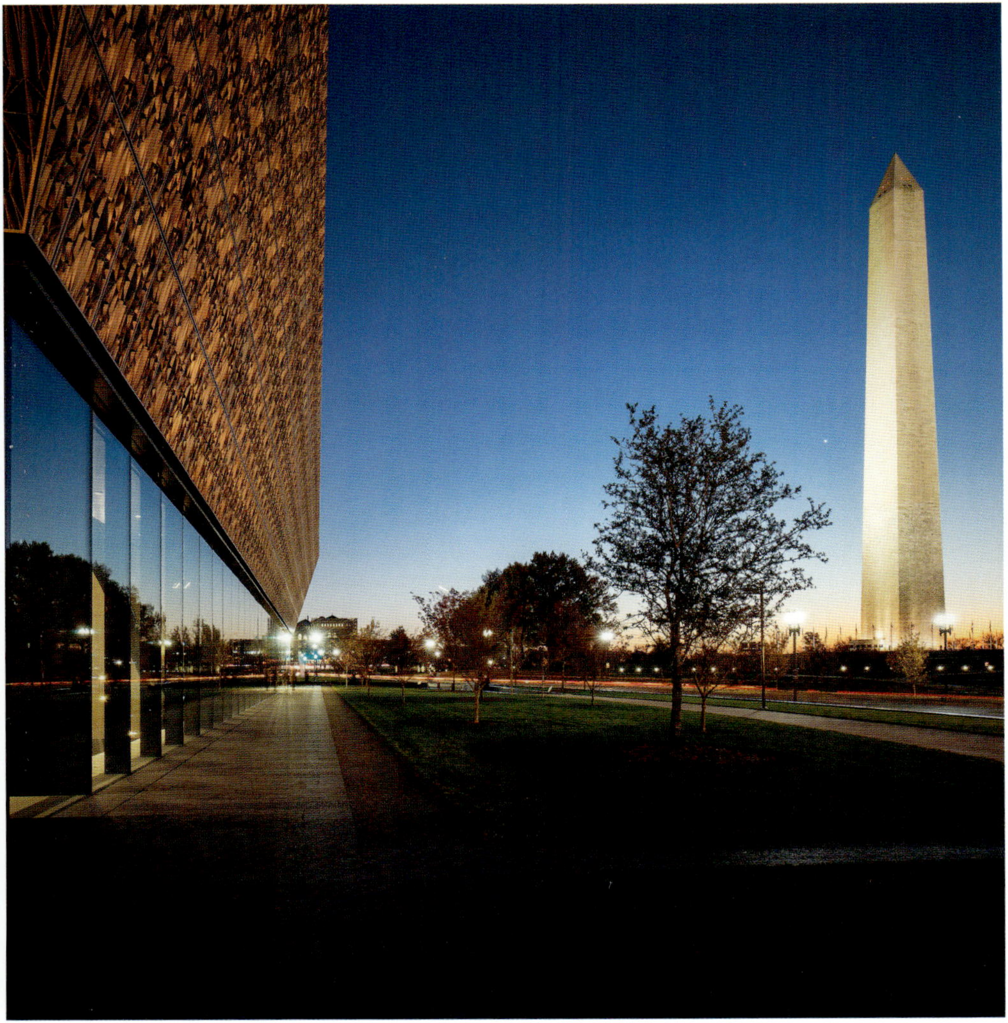

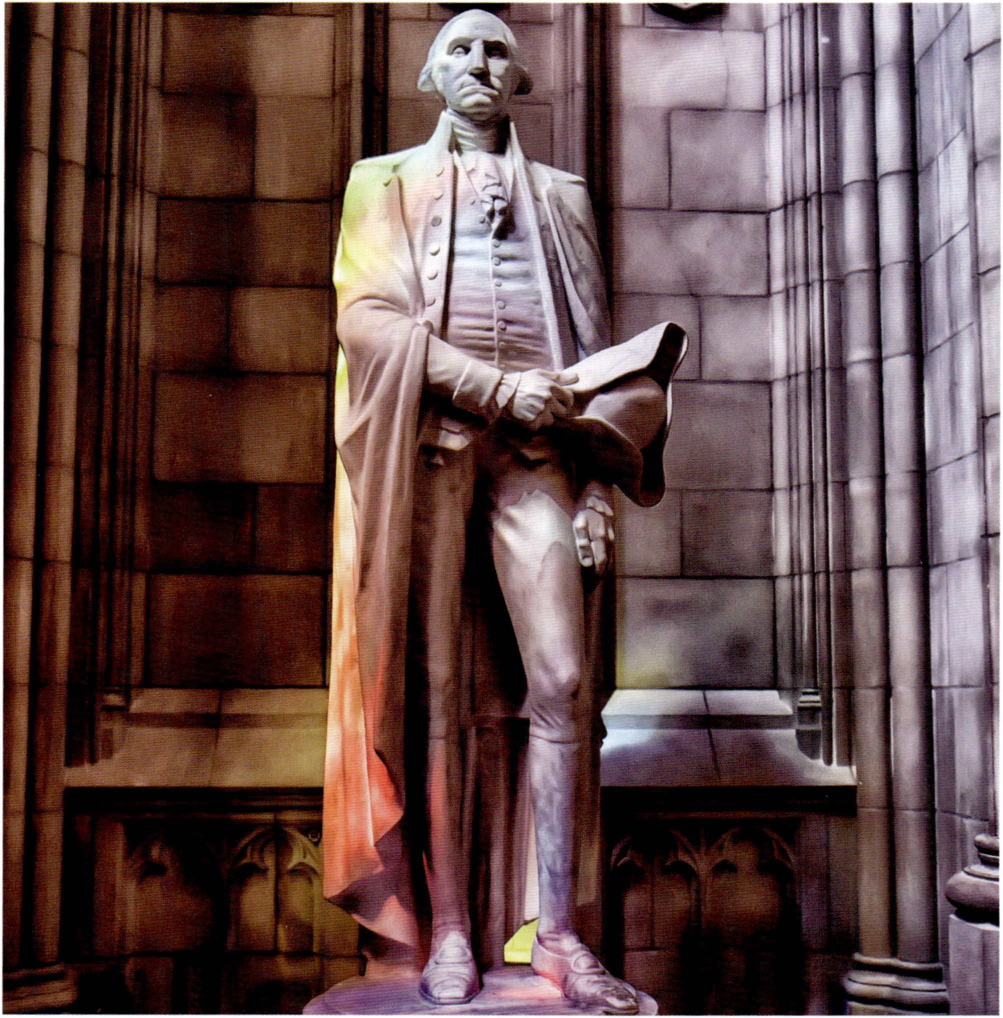

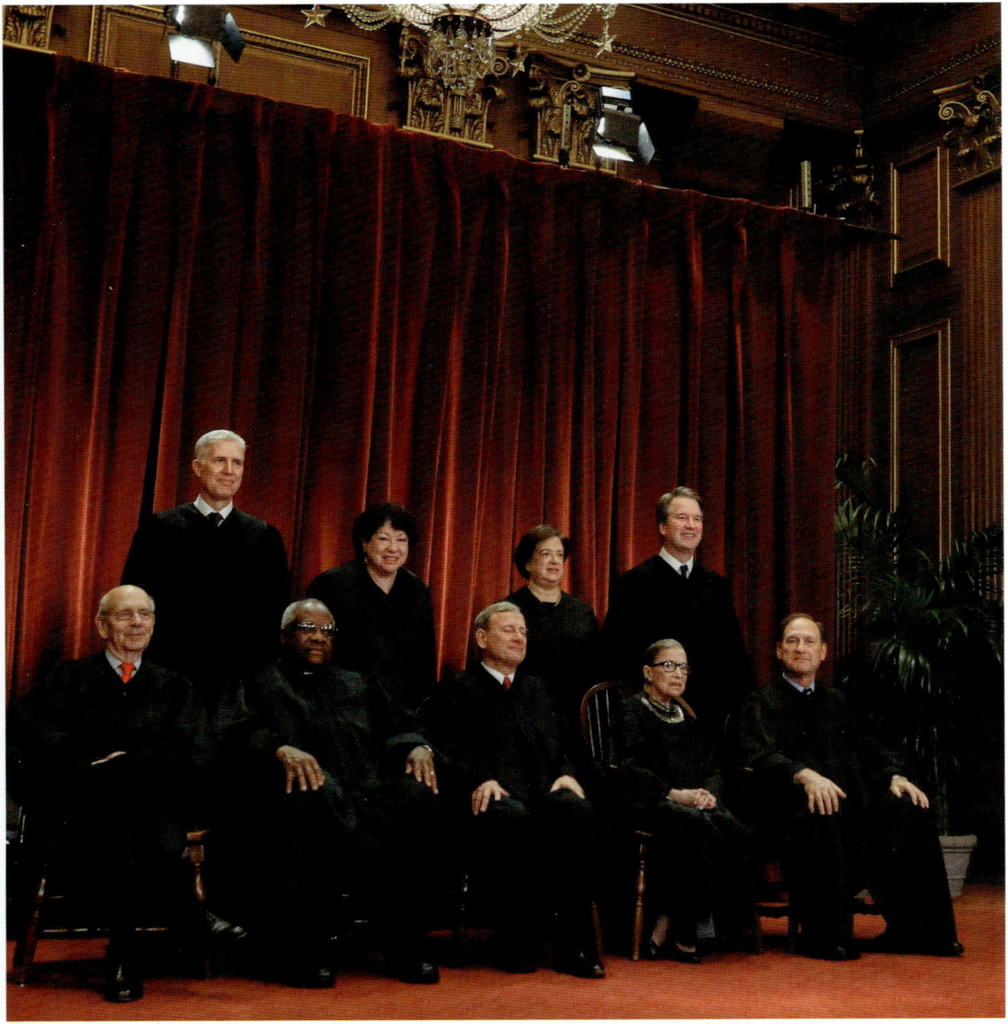

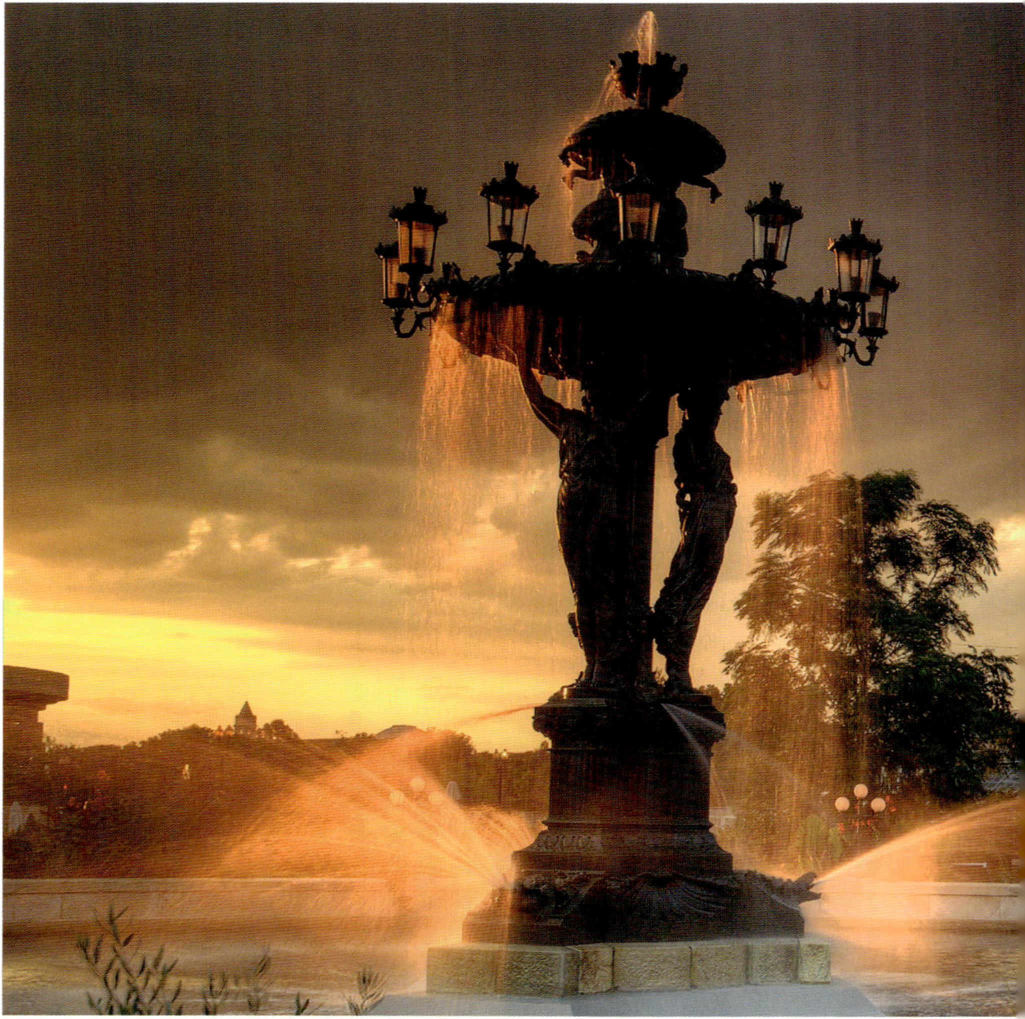

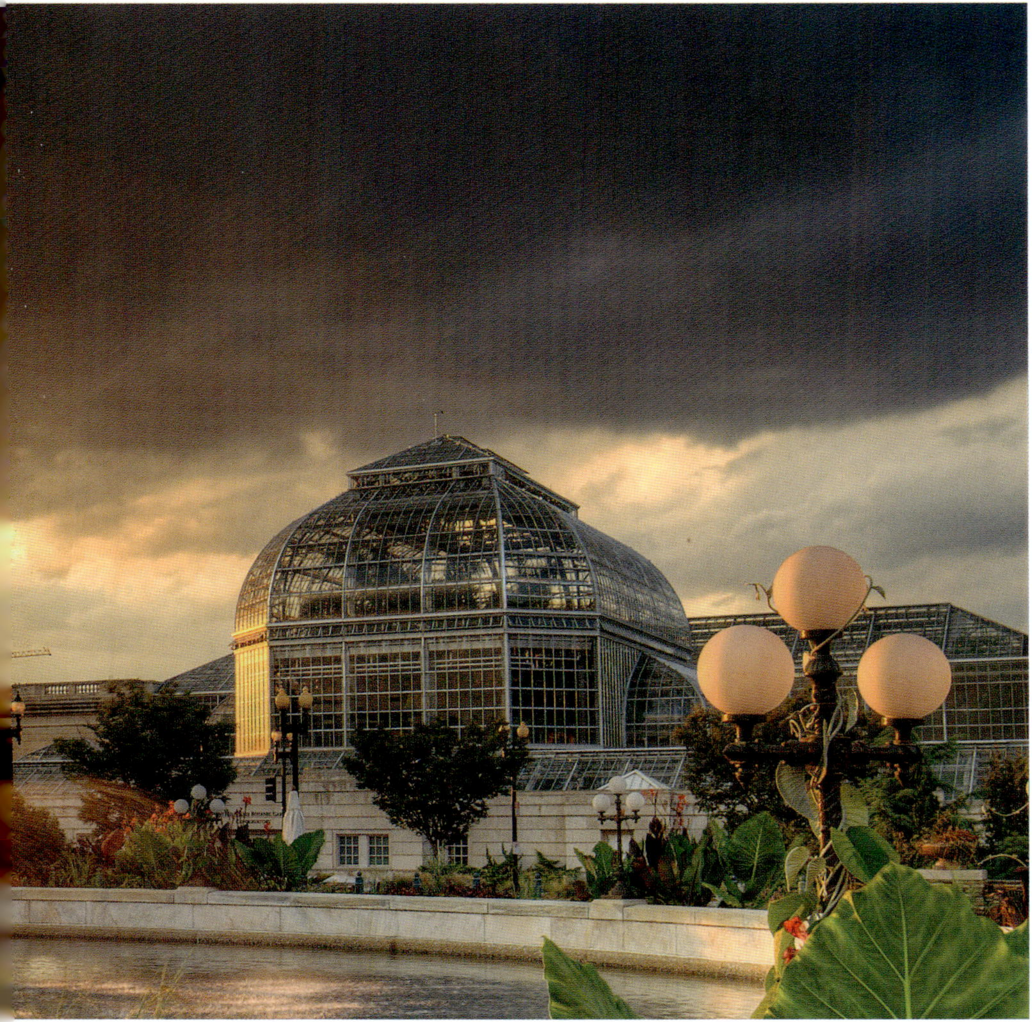

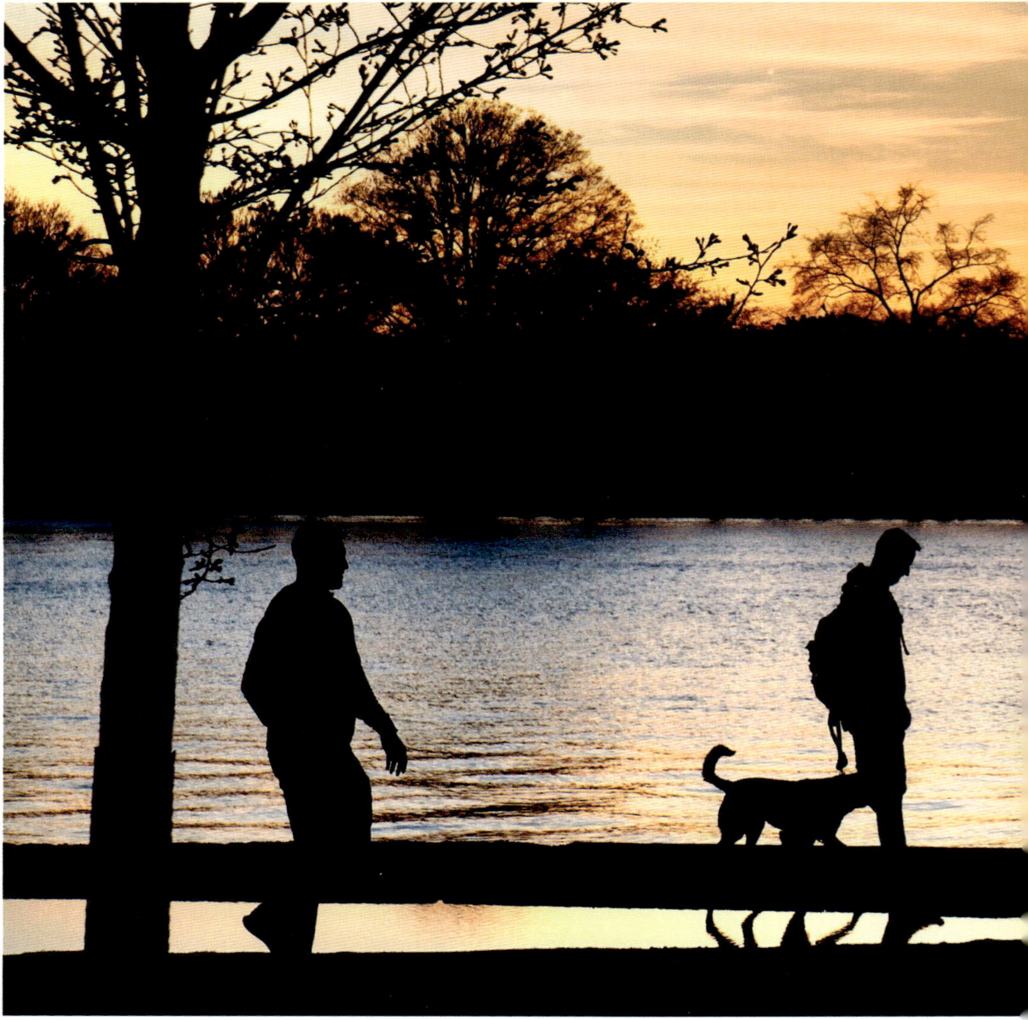

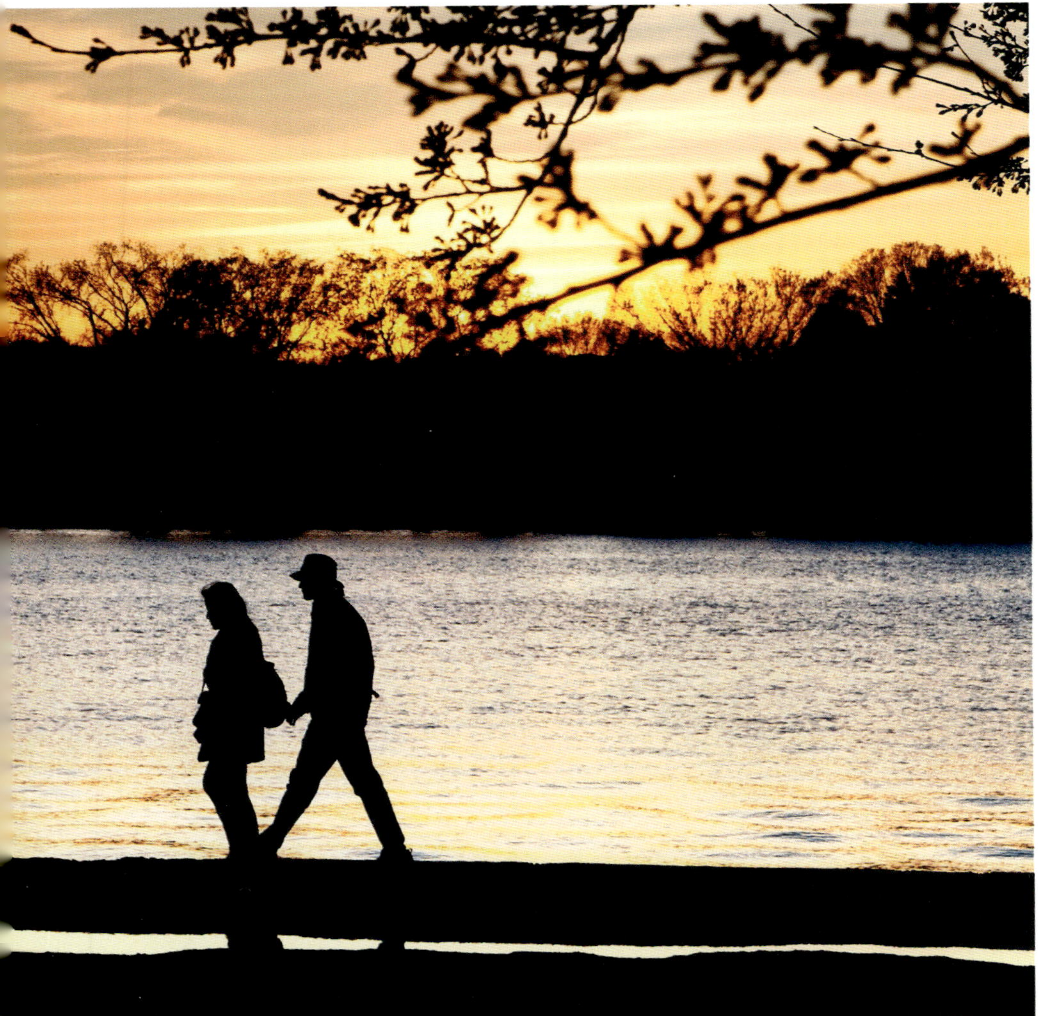

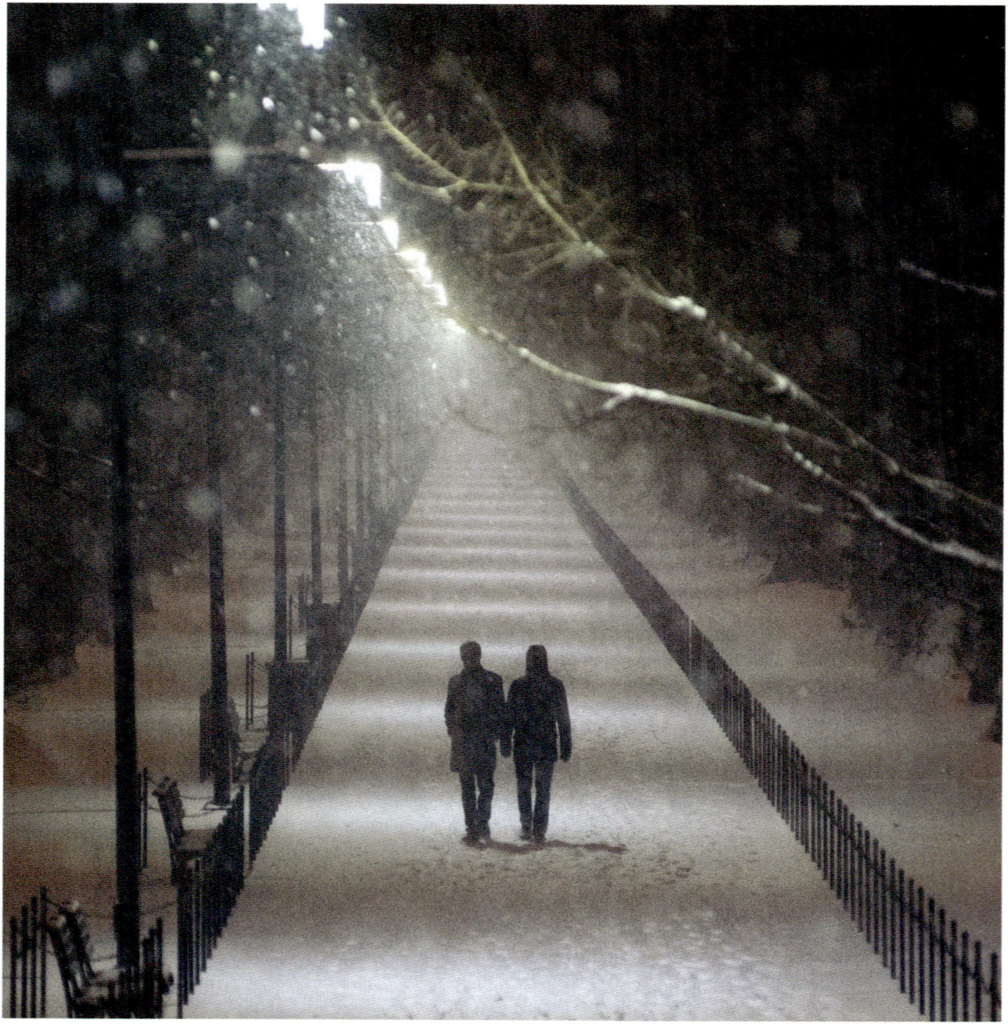

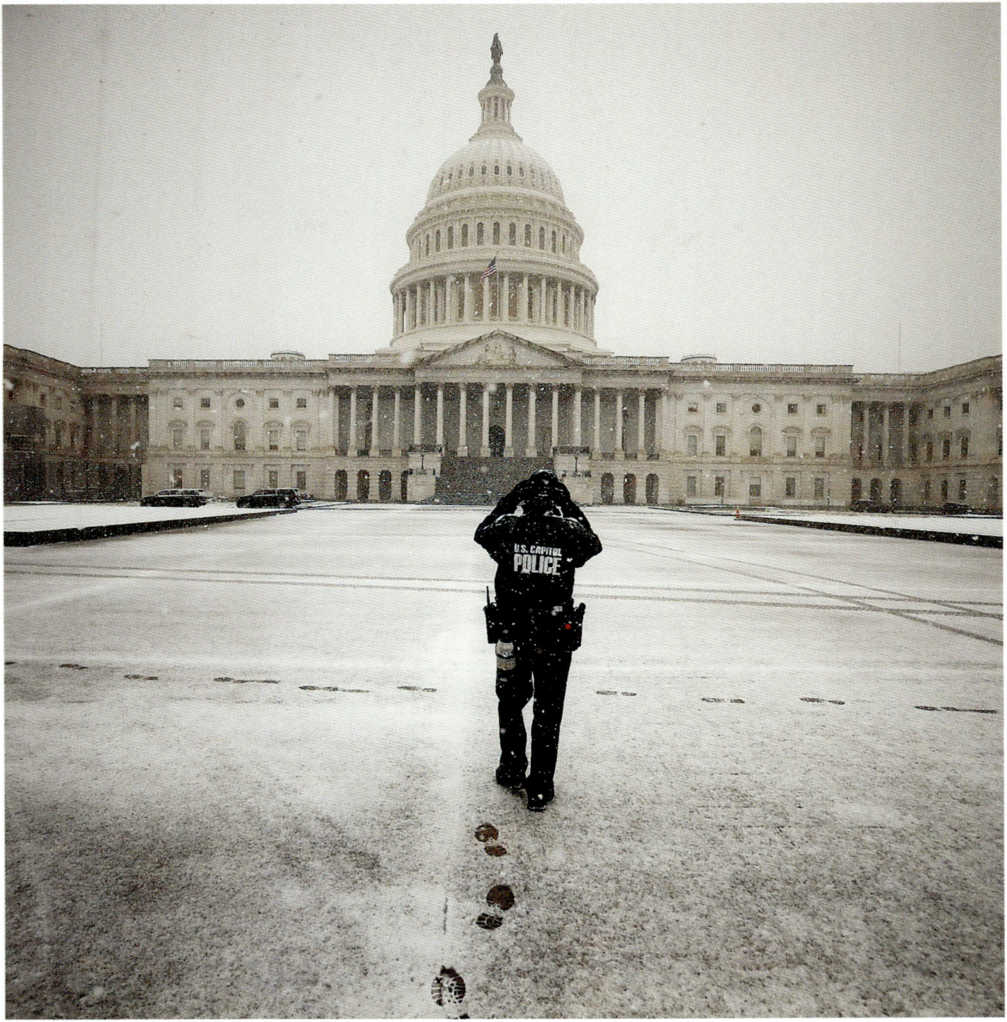
U.S. CAPITOL
POLICE

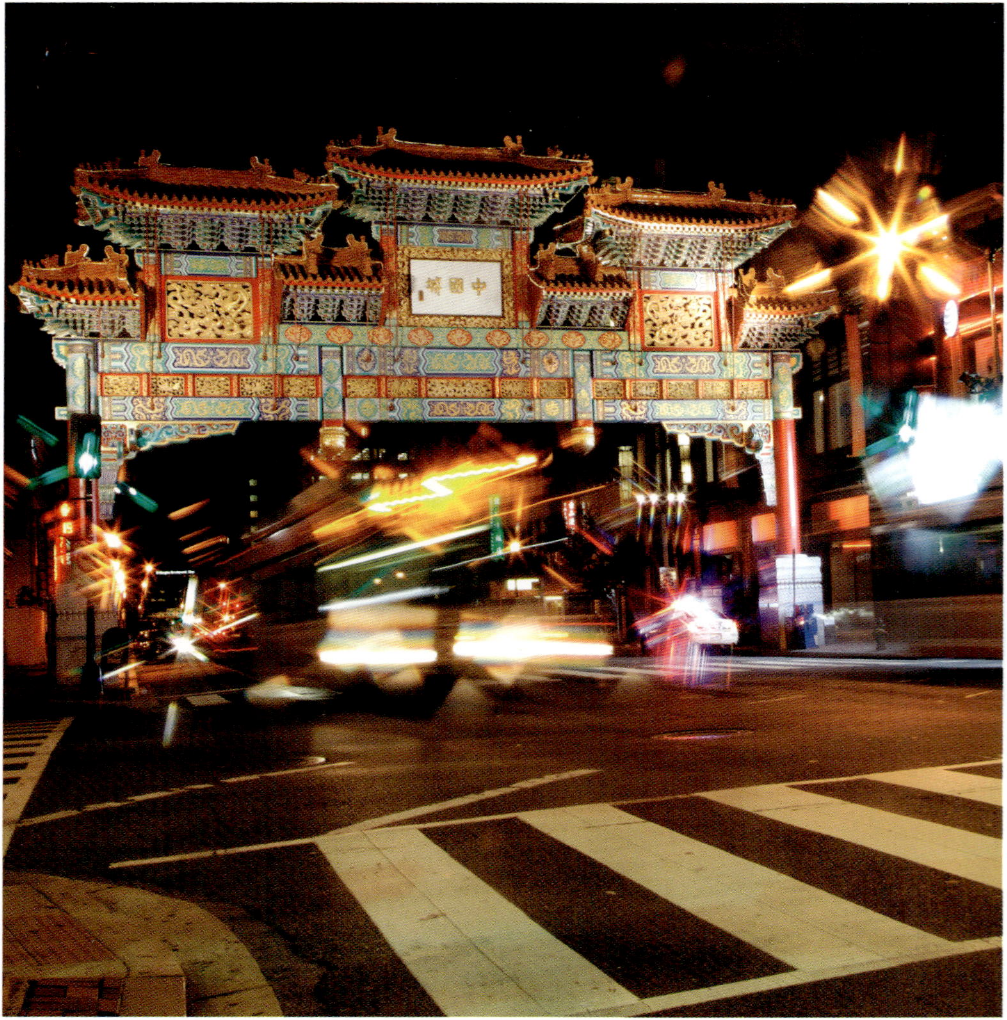
中國城

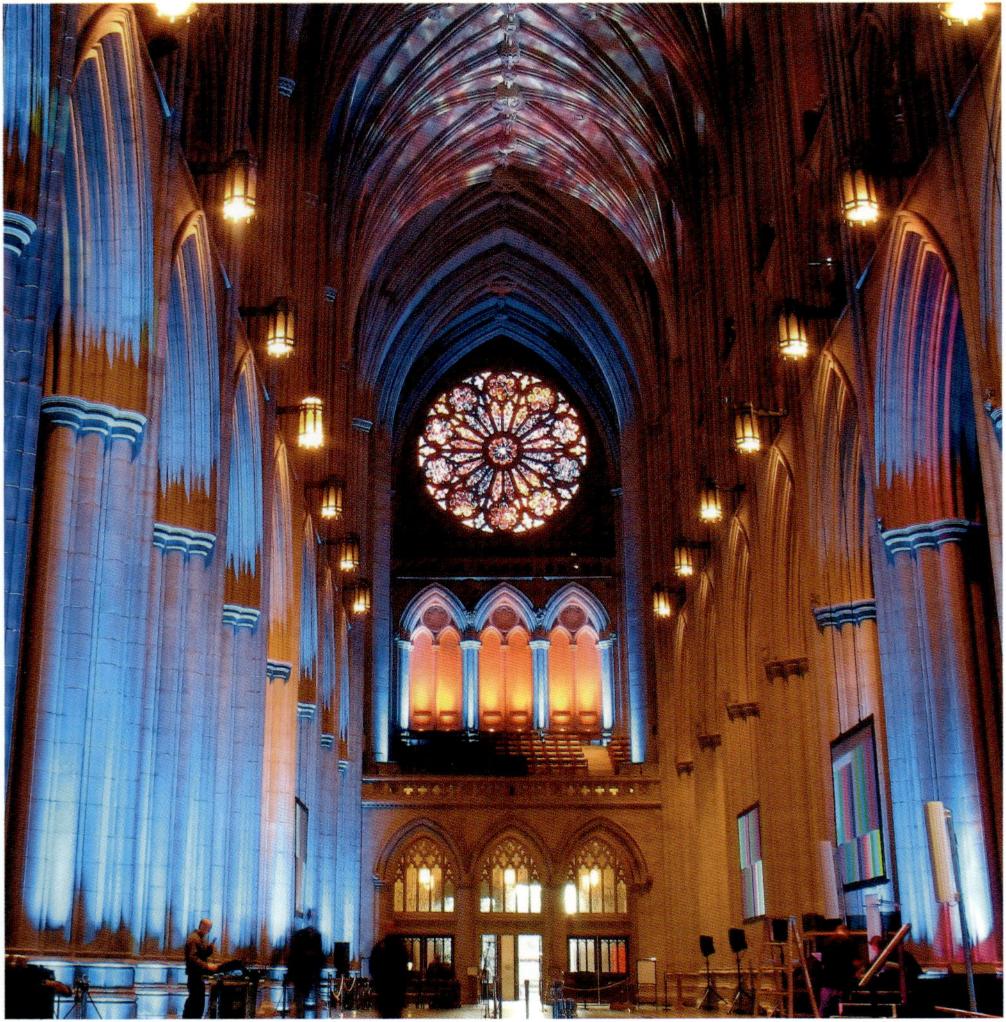

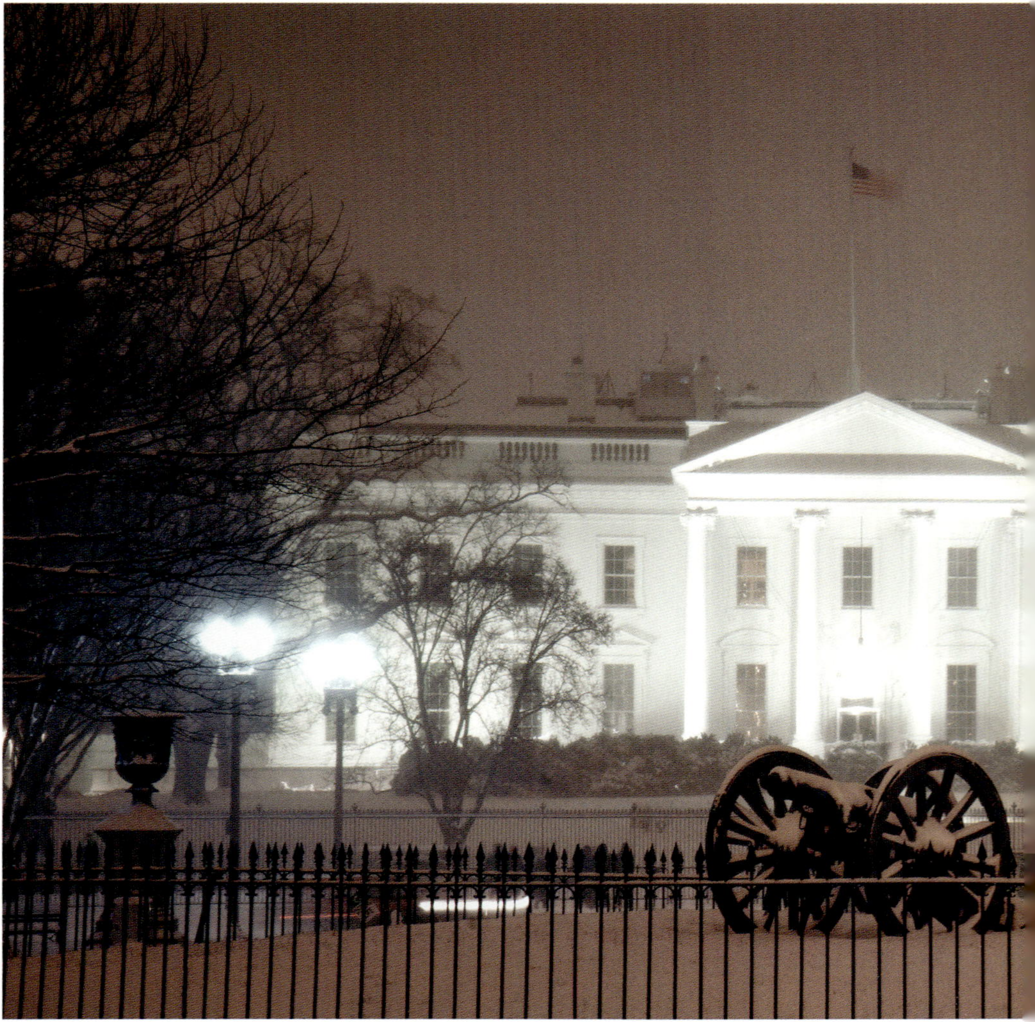

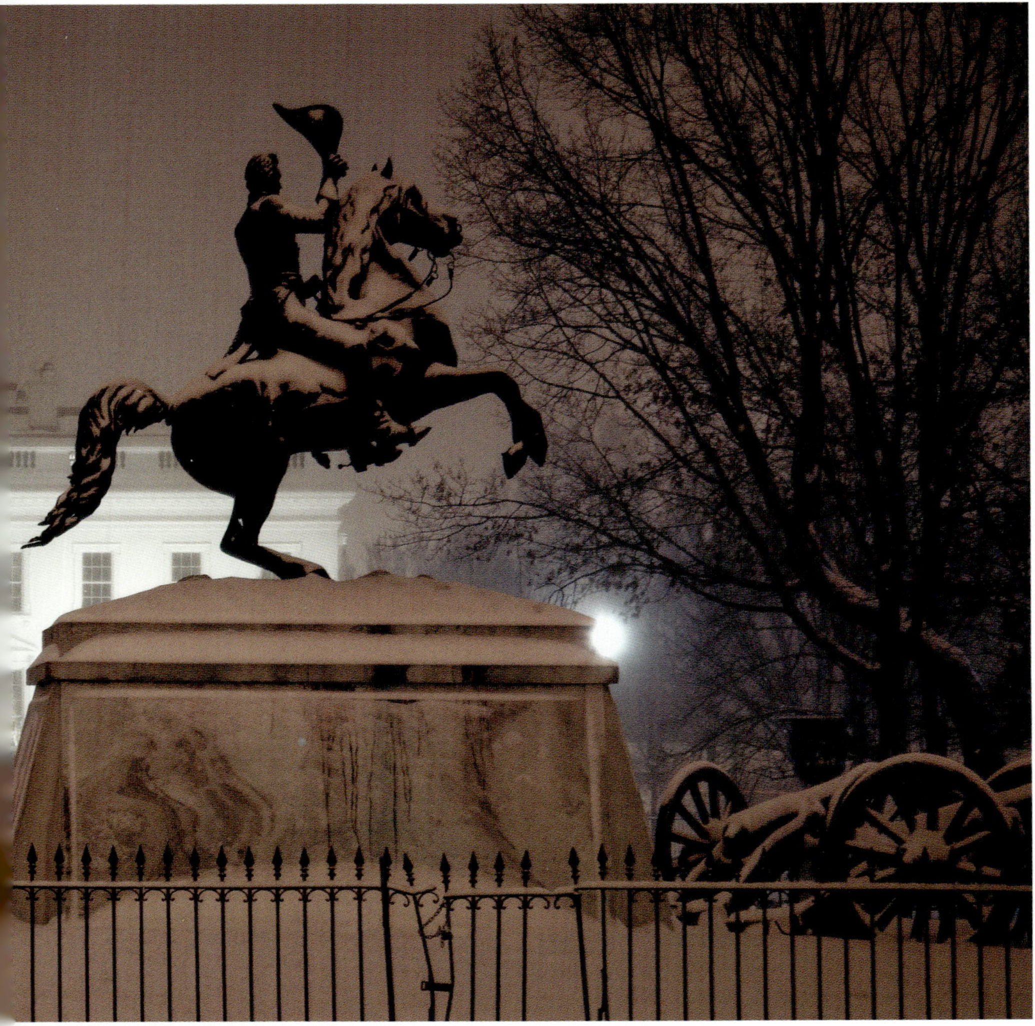

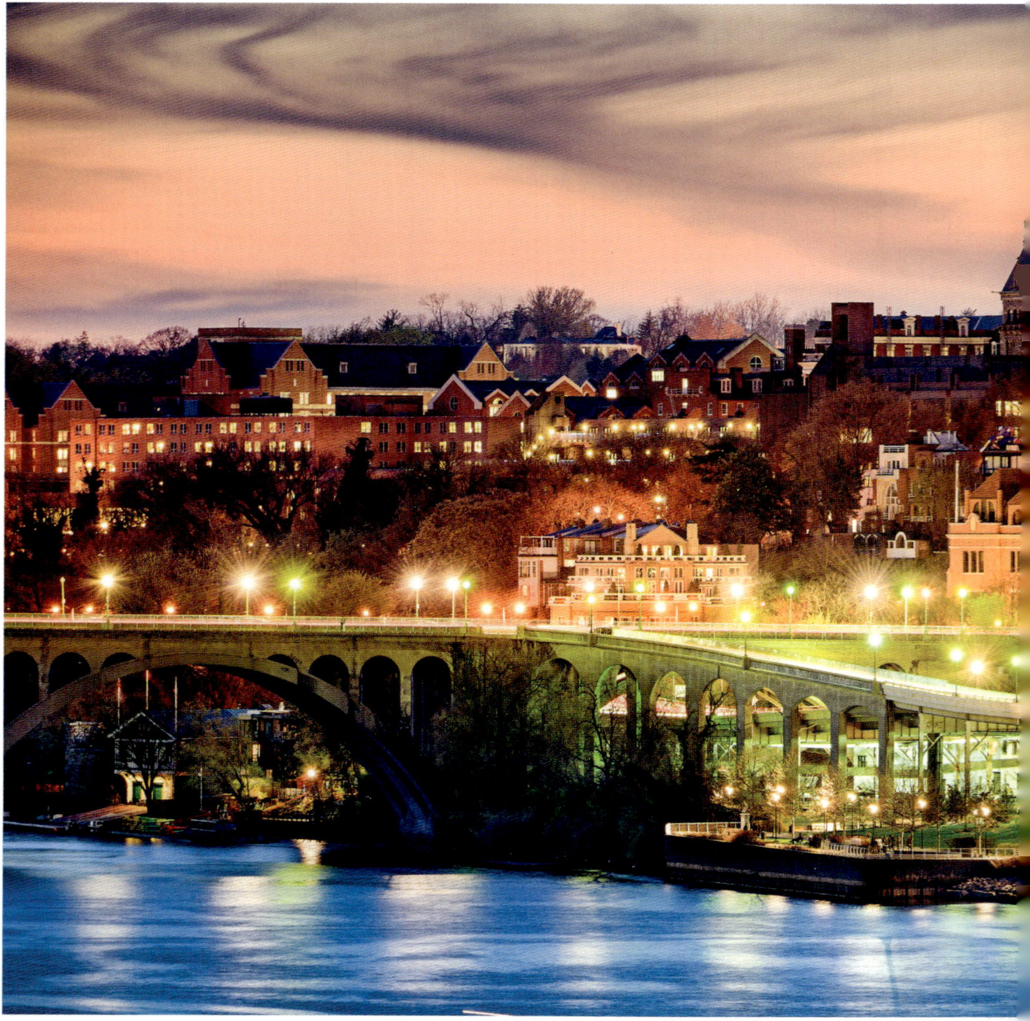

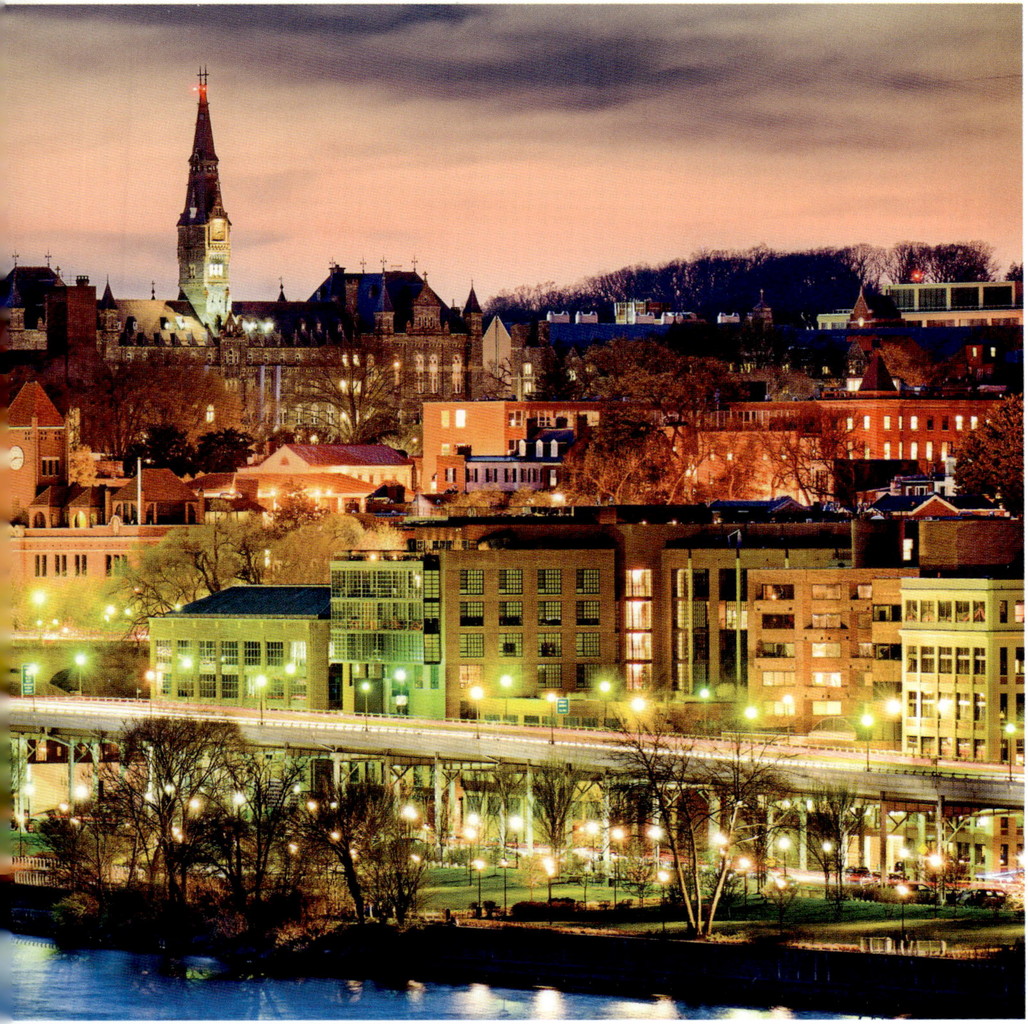

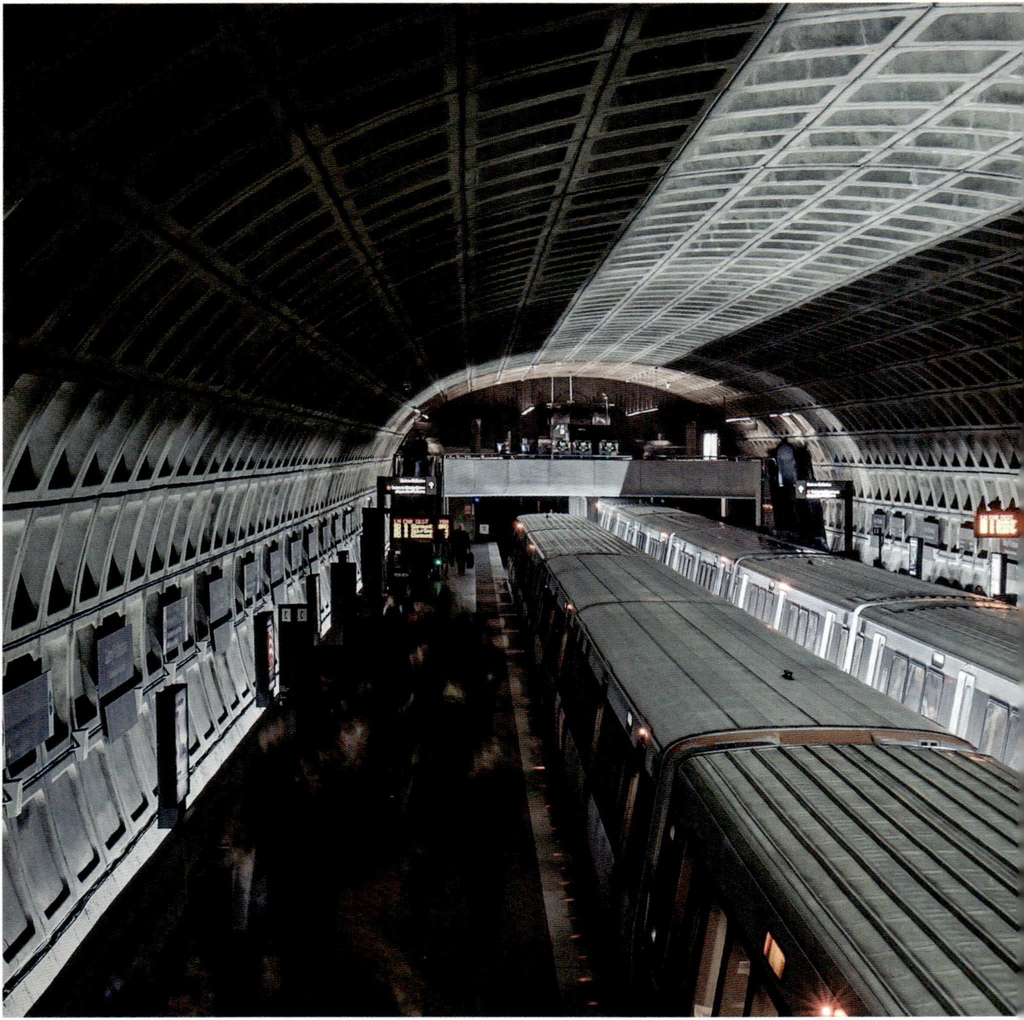

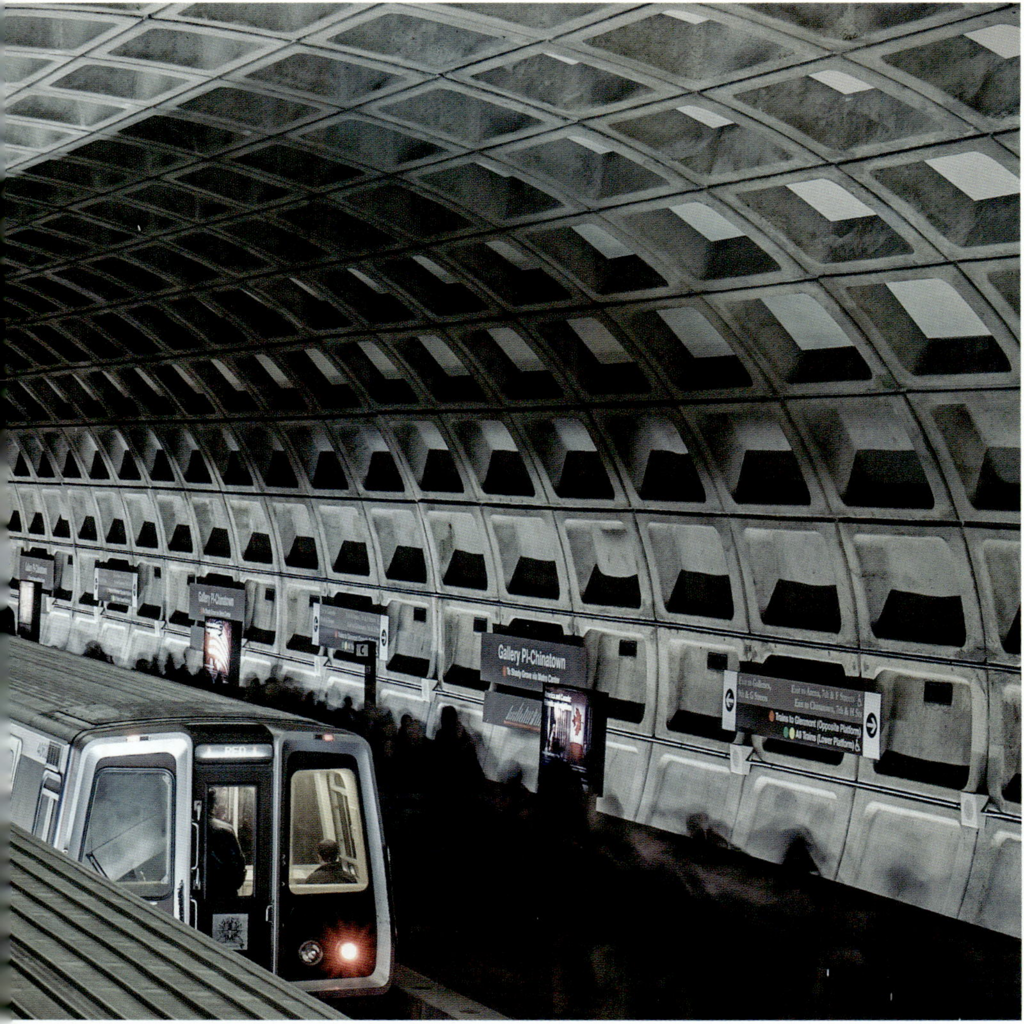
Gallery Pl-Chinatown

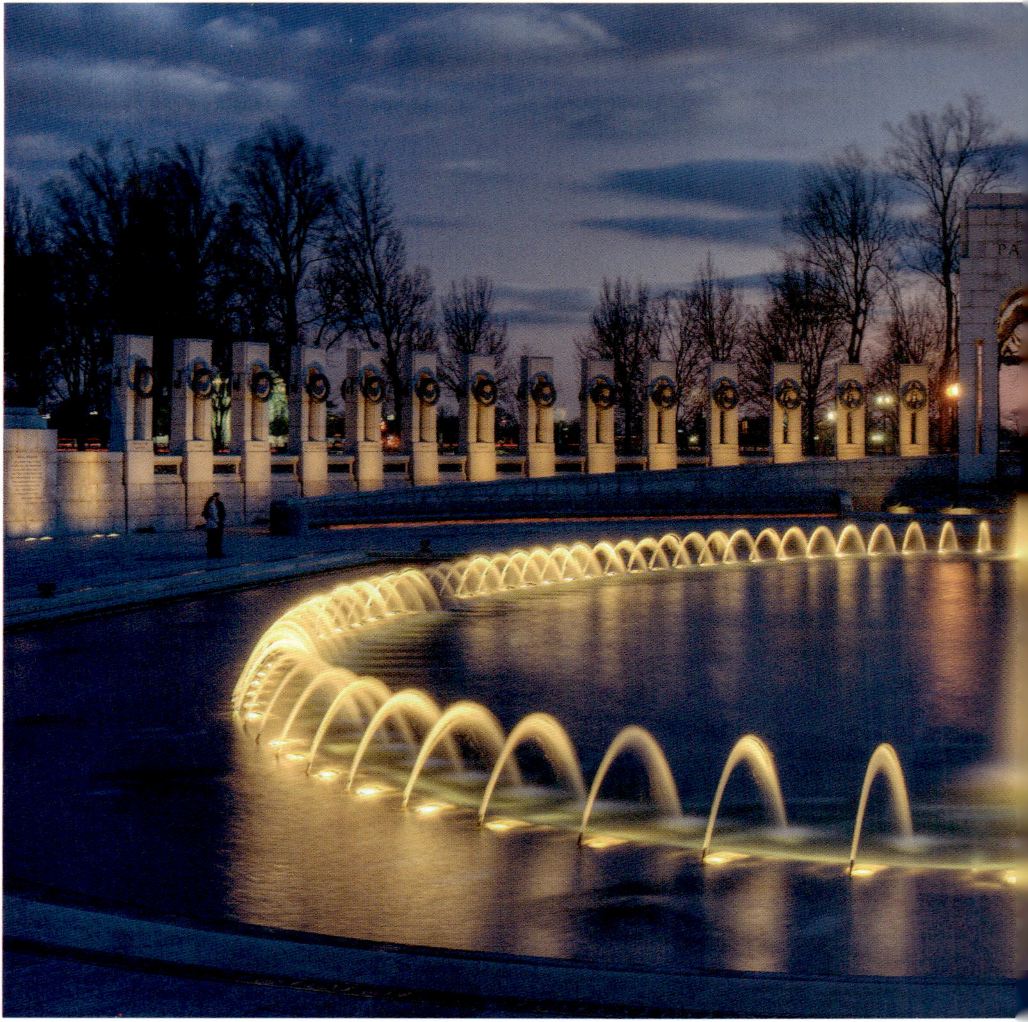

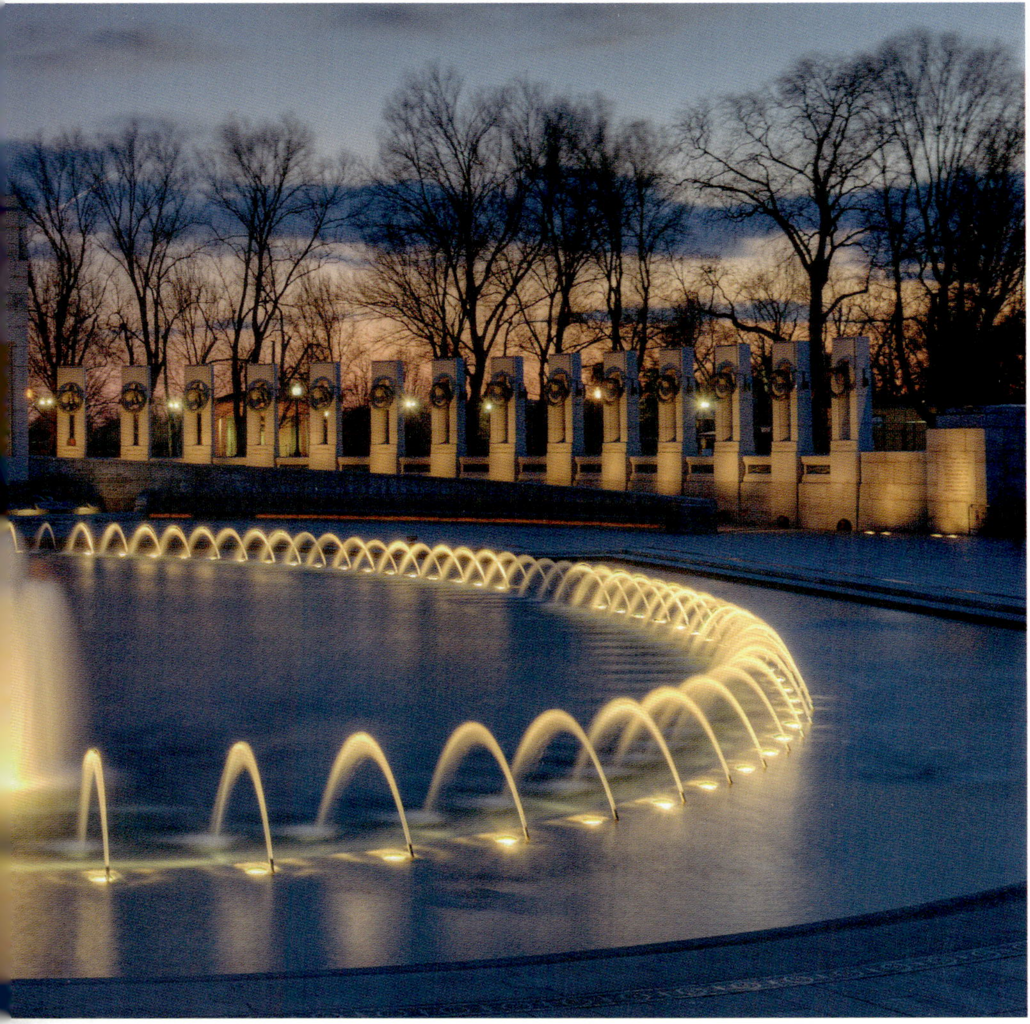

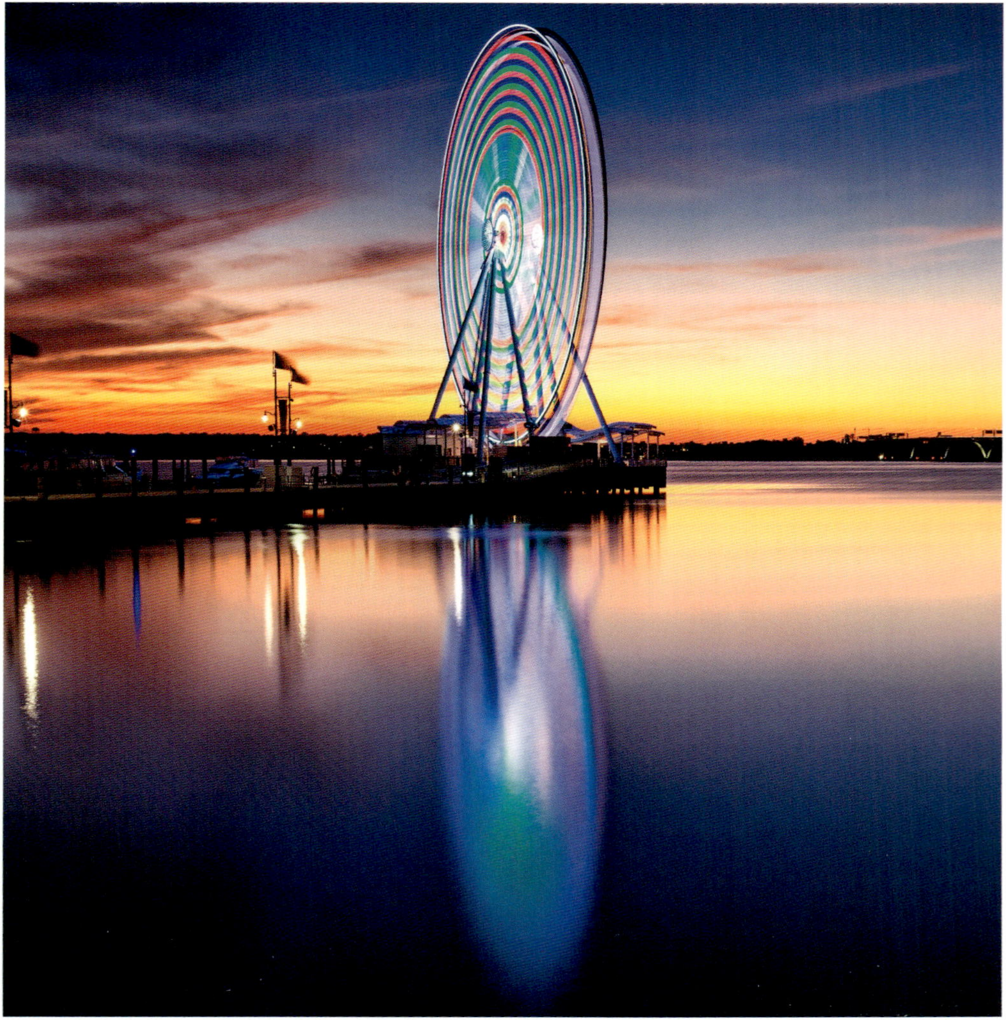

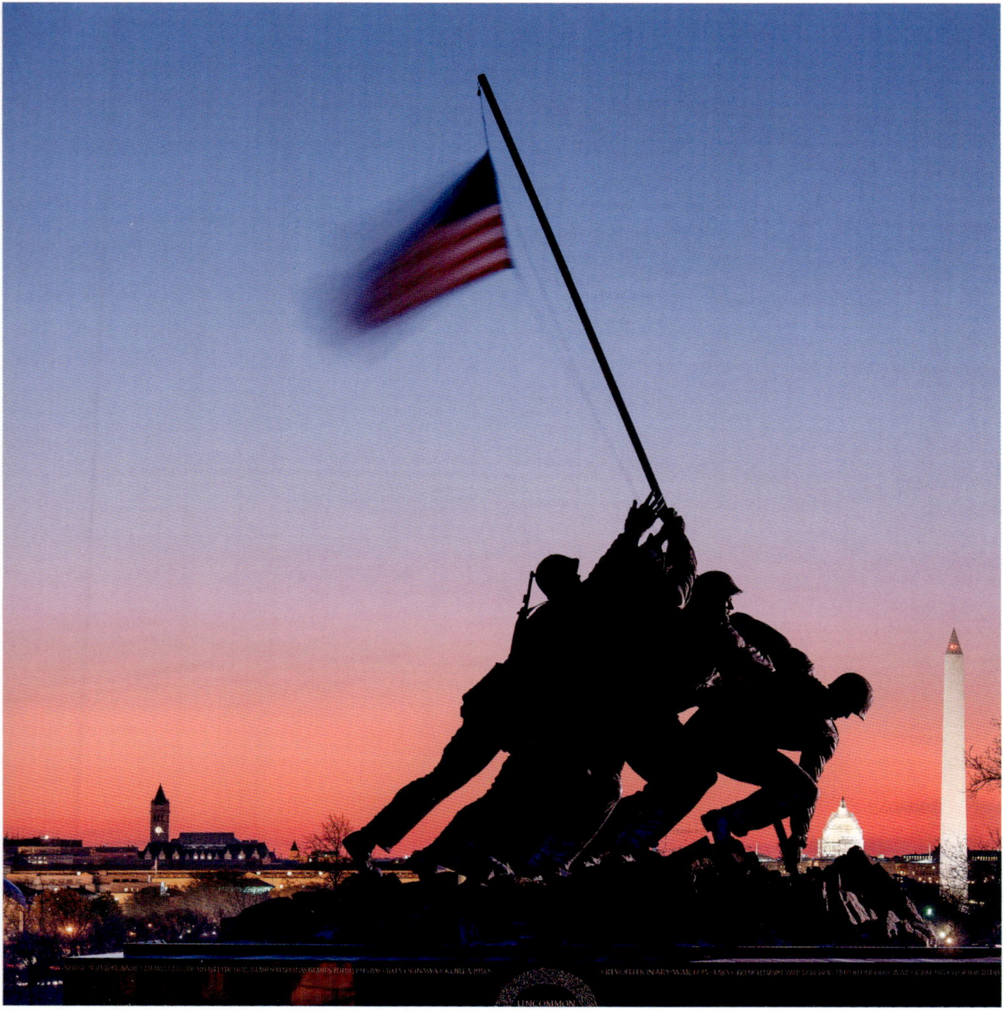
UNCOMMON

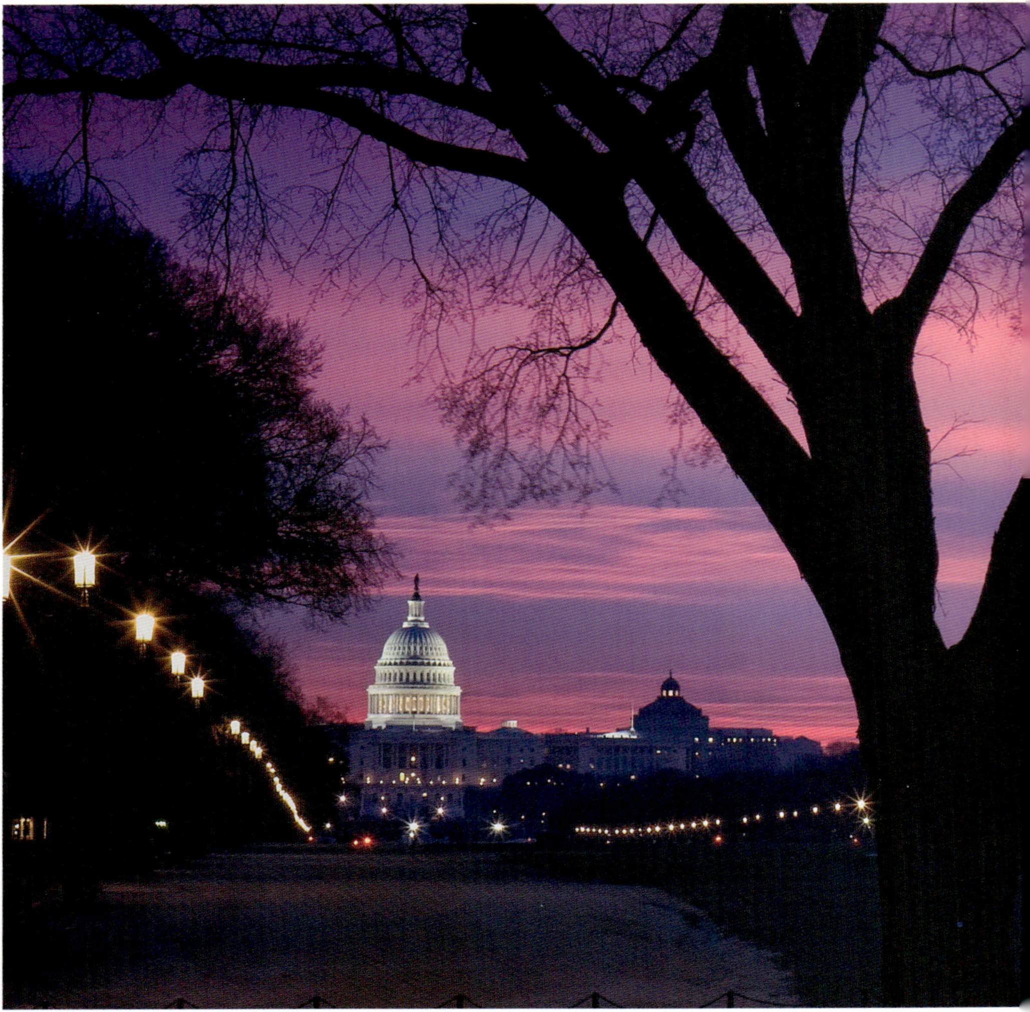

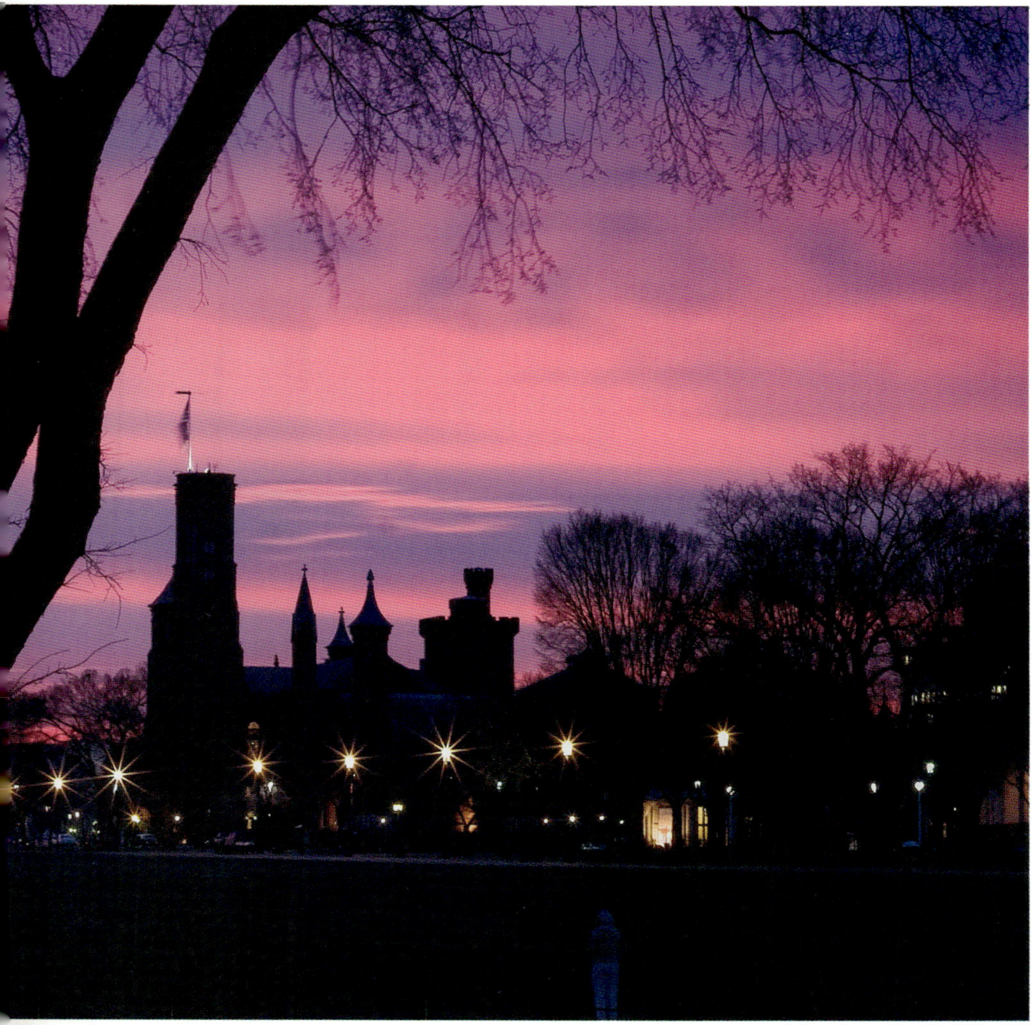

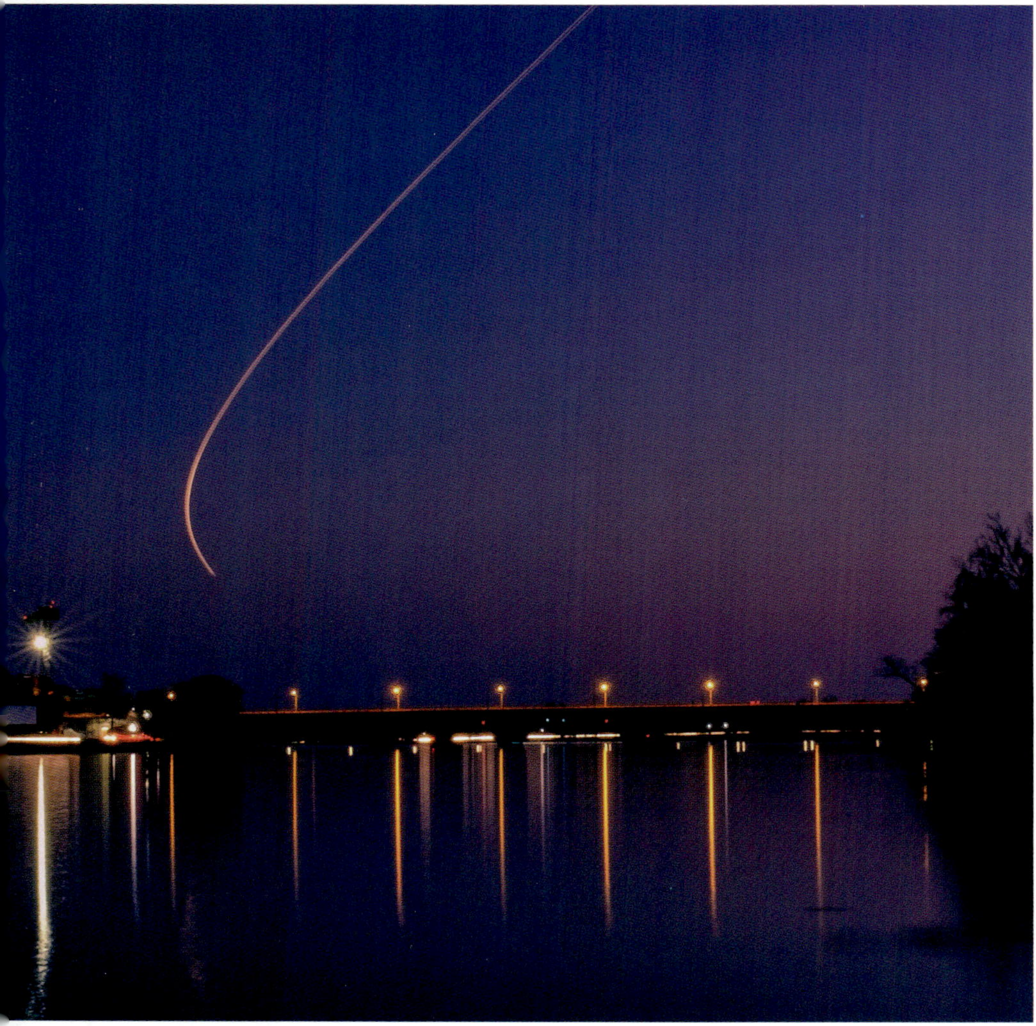

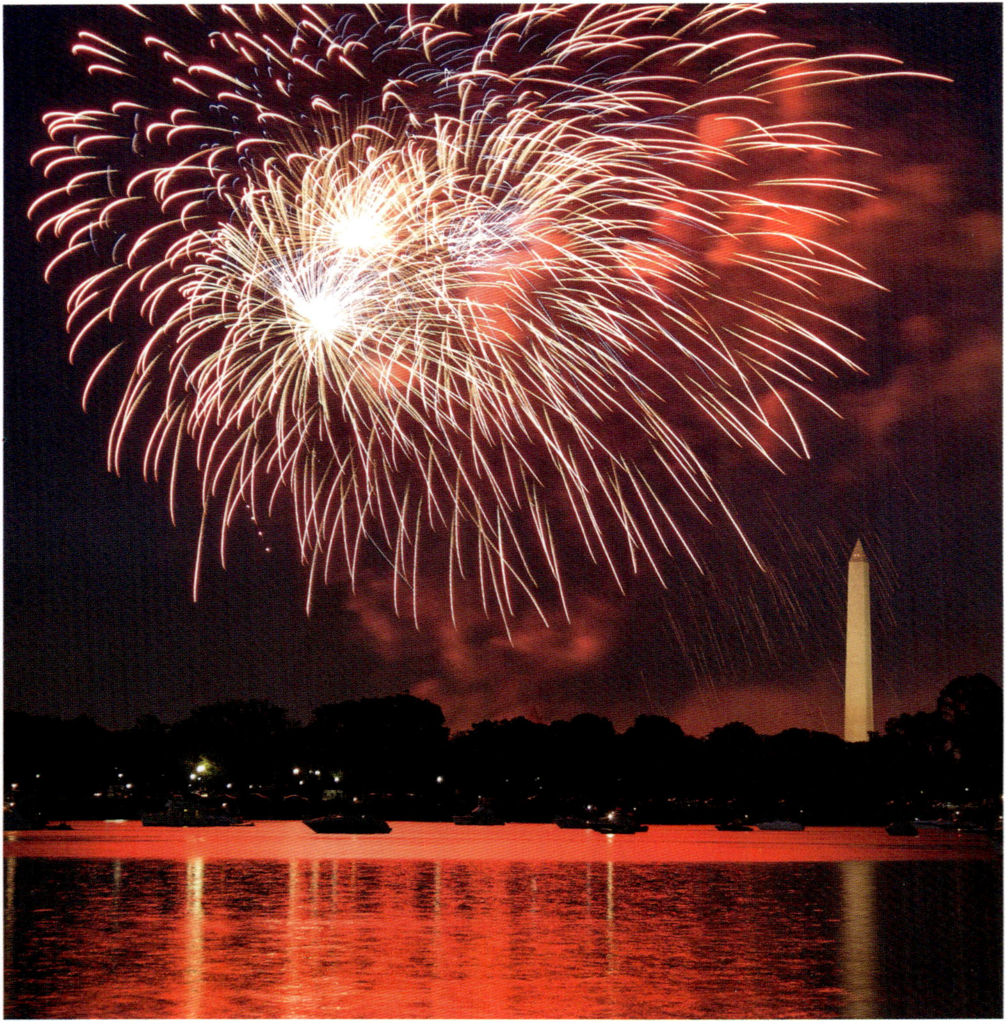

CAPTIONS

Front Cover: The Washington Monument at sunrise as seen from the Lincoln Memorial in Washington, DC.

Back Cover: A giant panda at the National Zoo.

Endsheets: The Capitol during the US Bicentennial.

6: A runner on a cloudy day near the Capitol Building.

7: The Lincoln Memorial at sunrise.

8-9: A view of the Jefferson Memorial during the National Cherry Blossom Festival.

10: The sun reflects off of the USS *Barry* destroyer at the Washington Navy Yard.

11: A Georgetown University crew prepares to set their boat in the water.

12: Jason Whitaker slides down the leg of *The Awakening,* a statue located along the Potomac River.

13: A view of the Jefferson Memorial from across the Tidal Basin.

14-15: Visitors ride bicycles along the Tidal Basin as Washington's famous cherry blossoms are in full bloom.

16-17: A bushel of blue crabs.

18-19: Tourists stand under cherry trees as spring blooms in Washington, DC.

20: Interior view of the dome inside the Capitol Building.

21: Challenger, a bald eagle, is released during an event with the Secretary of the Interior.

22: Tourists at Albert Einstein Memorial, a monumental bronze statue by sculptor Robert Berks located in the southwest corner of the National Academy of Sciences near the Vietnam Veterans Memorial.

23: Former presidents, vice presidents, first ladies, and President Donald Trump attend the state funeral of President George H.W. Bush at the National Cathedral on December 05, 2018.

24: An 8-month-old black Labrador retriever relaxes near the Tidal Basin.

25: A worker ices shrimp at a fish market on the Potomac River.

26: A close-up view of a statue at the Korean War Memorial.

27: Friends and family of Marine Chief Warrant Officer 3 Gary Stouffer watch as his casket is carried by a Marine Corps Honor Guard during a burial service at Arlington National Cemetery.

28: Customers order from colorful food trucks selling a variety of international cuisines lined up on the Mall in Washington, DC.

29: Spiced and steamed crabs from the Chesapeake Bay.

30: Ben's Chili Bowl, a landmark Washington restaurant founded in 1958.

31: A hot dog from Ben's Chili Bowl.

32-33: An aerial view of buildings around Dupont Circle.

34-35: Visitors enjoy the National Air and Space Museum of the Smithsonian Institution in Washington, DC.

36: Rowers push through heavy fog in Washington, DC.

37: Senate Bean Soup is a traditional dish served daily in the dining room of the United States Senate.

38-39: Large crowds gather at the Capitol during President Obama's inauguration on January 21, 2013.

40: *Marine One* approaches the White House.

41: The stunning fountain in Dupont Circle on a windy autumn day.

42-43: A Park Service employee cleans the Abraham Lincoln statue at the Lincoln Memorial.

44: Visitors peruse the Main Hall of the National Museum of Natural History.

45: A view of the impressive spiral staircase of the Supreme Court of the United States on Capitol Hill.

46: A F/A-18 Hornet flies over the Pentagon.

47: A man places his hand on the Vietnam Veterans Memorial where the names of 58,000 Americans killed in the Vietnam War are listed.

48: The National Museum of the American Indian.

49: An aerial view of Washington, DC, and the Potomac River.

50-51: A display of photographs inside the United States Holocaust Memorial Museum.

52-53: An aerial view of the fountain in the National Gallery of Art Sculpture Garden.

54: A close-up of a statue outside the United States Supreme Court.

55: A statue honoring Martin Luther King Jr. in Washington, DC.

56: A child sleds down the hill outside the US Capitol.

57: The Changing of the Guard at the Tomb of the Unknown Soldier in Arlington National Cemetery.

58: Leaves change color as autumn arrives in the Georgetown neighborhood of Washington, DC.

59: The fountain at the World War II Memorial sparkles in the sunlight.

60-61: A young woman overlooks the Potomac River near the Francis Scott Key Bridge at sunset.

62: A meeting of the House of Representatives.

63: A jogger runs through several inches of snow in front of the Jefferson Memorial.

64: Rowhouses in Washington, DC.

65: The National Museum of African American History and Culture at sunset.

66: Statue of George Washington inside the National Cathedral.

67: US Supreme Court Justices pose for an official portrait in November 2018.

68-69: A sunset view of the Bartholdi Fountain.

70-71: Visitors enjoy a spring evening along the Potomac River.

72: A couple walk hand in hand down a snowy path along the Mall.

73: A US Capitol Police Officer patrols the Capitol plaza as snow falls.

74: The Friendship Archway at Gallery Place/Chinatown in Washington, DC.

75: The sanctuary of the National Cathedral lit up in preparation for the Centennial celebration.

76-77: A view of the White House following a snowstorm.

78-79: The Georgetown skyline along the Potomac River.

80-81: Two Metro trains stop for passengers at Union Station.

82-83: The fountain at the World War II Memorial at dusk.

84: The Capital Wheel at National Harbor on the Potomac River in Maryland, just outside Washington, DC.

85: Marine Corps War Memorial at dawn.

86-87: View of the Mall and the Capitol Building in Washington, DC.

88-89: The Kennedy Center lights up the Potomac River.

90: Fireworks near the Washington Monument.

CREDITS

Front Cover: lucky-photographer/iStock/
Getty Images

Back Cover: Nick Pecker/Moment RF/
Getty Images

Endsheets: Joe Sohm/Digital Vision/
Getty Images

6: Cami Schmidt/EyeEm/Getty Images

7: Eric Felton/Moment/Getty Images

8-9: F11photo/Shutterstock

10: Joseph Gruber/Editorial RF/Getty Images

11: LBeaumont/iStock/Getty Images

12: Mark Wilson/Getty Images News/
Getty Images

13: SKLA/iStock/Getty Images

14-15: Wavebreak Media/iStock/Getty Images

16-17: Brian Clay/iStock/Getty Images

18-19: Mark Wilson/Getty Images News/
Getty Images

20: Allan Baxter/DigtialVision/Getty Images

21: Win McNamee/Getty Images News/
Getty Images

22: Askolds Berovskis/Shutterstock

23: Chip Somodevilla/Getty Images News/
Getty Images

24: Joseph Gruber/Editorial RF/Getty Images

25: Brendan Smialowski/Getty Images News/
Getty Images

26: Byron Key/Shutterstock

27: Win McNamee/Getty Images News/
Getty Images

28: LazyLlama/Shutterstock

29: Cyndi Monaghan/Moment/Getty Images

30: Joaquin Ossorio Castillo/Shutterstock

31: Robert Crow/Shutterstock

32-33: GlowImages/Getty Images

34-35: Sean Pavone/Shutterstock

36: Orhan Cam/Shutterstock

37: Alexandra Grablewski/DigitalVision/
Getty Images

38-39: Eliyahu Yosef Parypa/Shutterstock

40: Zach Gibson/Getty Images News/
Getty Images

41: Jaime Montemayor/Shutterstock

42-43: Mark Wilson/Getty Images News/
Getty Images

44: Kamira/Shutterstock

45: CHBD/iStock/Getty Images

46: Everett Historical/Shutterstock

47: Spencer Platt/Getty Images News/
Getty Images

48: Larry Mayer/Stockbyte/Getty Images

49: Stocktrek/DigitalVision/Getty Images

50-51: GiuseppeCrimeni/Shutterstock

52-53: Pavel L Photo and Video/Shutterstock

54: flySnow/iStock/Getty Images

55: Ruben Martinez Barricarte/Shutterstock

56: Chip Somodevilla /Staff/Getty
Images News

57: Worawat Dechatiwong/Shutterstock

58: Chemistkane/iStock/Getty Images

59: Skyhobo/iStock/Getty Images

60-61: Ablokhin/iStock/Getty Images

62: Ftwitty/iStock/Getty Images

63: Mark Wilson/Getty Images News/
Getty Images

64: Roberson Photos/Moment/Getty Images

65: Steve Heap/Shutterstock

66: Evdoha_spb/Shutterstock

67: Chip Somodevilla/Getty Images News/
Getty Images

69: TomWachs/iStock/Getty Images

70-71: Sara Bernheisel/Moment/Getty Images

72: TomWachs/iStock/Getty Images

73: Mark Wilson/Getty Images News/
Getty Images

74: DKFielding/iStock/Getty Images

75: Coast-to-Coast/iStock/Getty Images

76-77: TomWachs/iStock/Getty Images

78-79: SeanPavonePhoto/iStock/Getty Images

80-81: Shakzu/iStock/Getty Images

82-83: TomWachs/iStock/Getty Images

84: photo by Edward Kreis, dK.i imaging/
Moment/Getty Images

85: Sean Pavone/Shutterstock

86-87: Lingbeek/E+/Getty Images

88-89: Tennisqiu/Shutterstock

90: robmbrown/Shutterstock

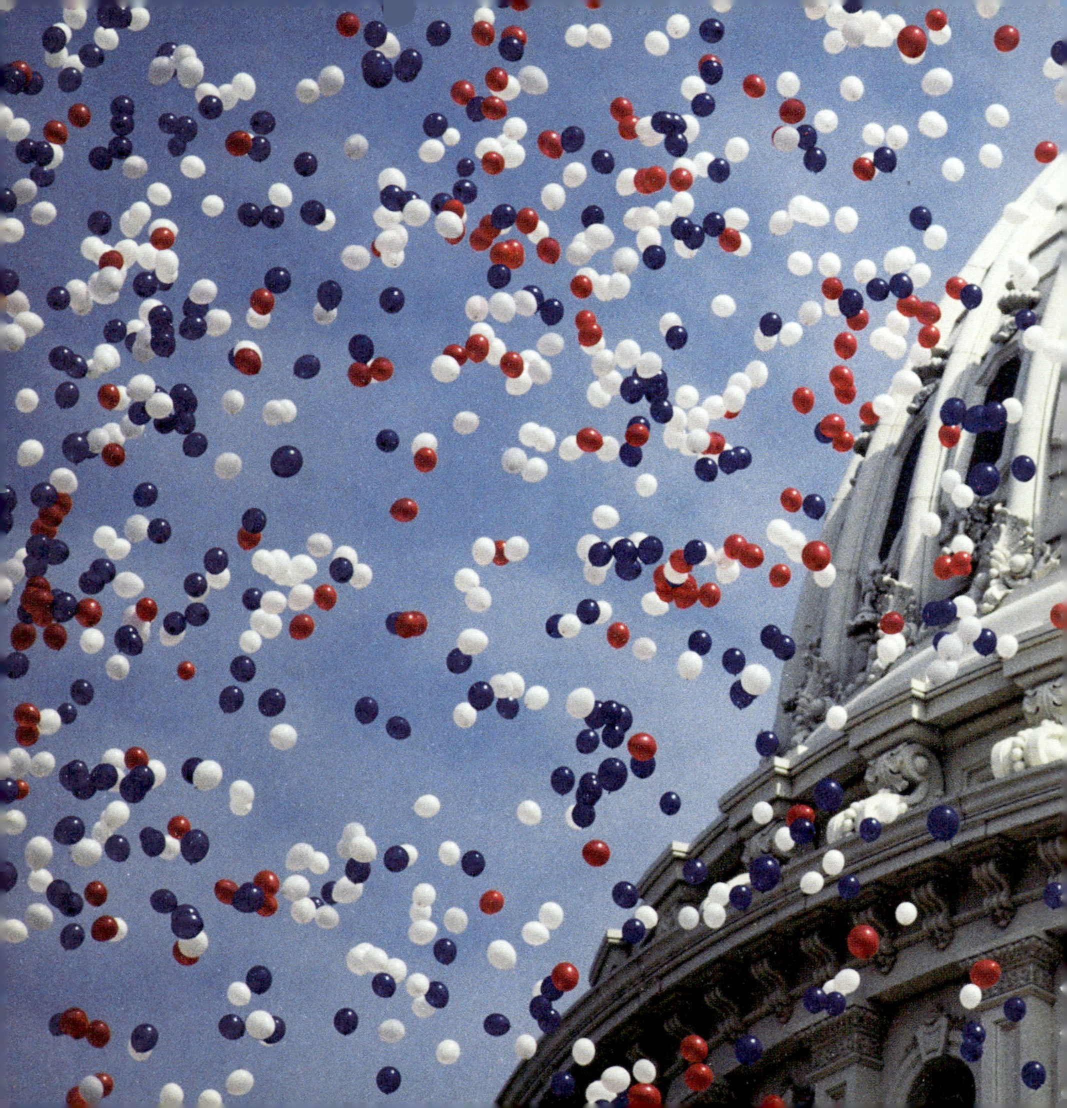